A Bird in the Hand

Ted Nelson Lundrigan

Illustrated by Bob White

Text copyright © 2006 by Ted Nelson Lundrigan
Illustrations copyright © 2006 by Bob White

Design by Lindy Gifford, Damariscotta, Maine

Printed by Versa Press, East Peoria, Illinois

5   4   3   2   1

ISBN 0-89272-722-5   (13-digit) 978-089272-722-3

Library of Congress Control Number: 2006924658

Countrysport Press
Camden, Maine
A division of Down East Enterprise, publisher of *Shooting Sportsman*
magazine.

To order a catalog or purchase a book, call 800-685-7962, or visit
www.countrysportpress.com

Introduction

I know that Lloyd wanted me to work the same magic. He had invited me to come to North Dakota and hunt pheasants on his home place. A friend had told him about the magazine article I wrote. Within a year of the article's publication, readers had filled the reservation book at the Cannonball Company in Regent, North Dakota.

But Lloyd Fugelstad's boyhood farm was not the same place at all. It was a preserve, and this was April. The pheasants were tired, tail-pecked, and accommodating creatures willing to hold for a pointing dog. My German shorthairs, hardened by wild birds and bored with winter, swept them up like biscuits on a hardwood floor.

The story was in the farm, Lloyd's life there, and in the nearby town of Luverne. I went through the motions of hunting and shooting and collecting game, but my enjoyment came from listening to his memories. Each draw and waterway, and every crop field, now picket-fenced in battered corn, was a page of his life. The square, two-story frame house and, next to it, the rusted cab of an old pickup sprouting weeds through its engine block held more interest for me than the birds Lloyd had collected with a fish net, then sprinkled here and there.

The Fugelstad family—nine of them—driving into Luverne on a Saturday evening. All the bunch, released onto the streets and under strict instruction to return by 10:30 P.M. These square-headed Midwesterners turned out to mingle with others until the coach would turn into a pumpkin. That was an image I could write about.

Now, only a brother remained on the farm with Lloyd and his mother. When I went up the dusty stairs of the old house and pushed open the dry, creaky door to my "room for the night," I expected to unbuckle my six-gun, hang it on a peg next to my chaps, then stretch out fully clothed on the squeaky iron-framed bed. Why not? Dust blew across the yard and rattled against the window panes. A wisp or two puffed under the sash. Downstairs, quiet voices returned the events of the day.

It wasn't quite the way I imagined—I had no pistol, cowboy boots, or chaps—but it was close enough. Lloyd's dream was still a work in progress. He had not reached the catalog-recommended, interior-designed ambiance of his competitors. Nor would he, because money fuels the recreational-hunting business, and certain things are expected by those who want a guaranteed return on their hunting dollar. Lloyd needed those paying customers because he was working hard to build a "hunting experience." His fields, his draws and corners, his crops were not real. They were, instead, a fiction; a playing field. The pheasants, if they lived through a day's shooting, were confounded by their new and alien surroundings and would most likely be eaten by the red tooth of nature. Tomorrow, new recruits would fill the gaps and the thin orange line of the harvesters would return. The birds' function was not to reproduce: it was to create a bang.

Far to the west, across the Missouri River and south through the rolling hills and buttes, the farmers and merchants and citizens of Regent were not content to let the hound dog of decay sleep in their streets. They organized. Farmers changed their practices and expanded the fence rows and waterways. Crops were raised, bailed, and hauled to pheasant wintering grounds along the river and in the shelterbelts. The pheasant became a cash crop to be harvested along with the wheat. Homes became bed-and-breakfasts, bird hunters were welcomed, and guests were entertained. The food plots became so filled with the pheasants that their numbers could not be counted.

I came, once, to write about what the people of Regent had created. They showed me, and I wrote, that the hand of man could create wild pheasants in such profusion that they were like feed-mill sparrows. I remember cresting a bank along the Cannonball River, and as I looked out over the field the surface of the ground moved. It slipped to the west in a fleeing, jumping, flying mass of birds more like a herd than a flock, like something that one would see in a film about African wildlife. In order to make my day last beyond ten minutes and three shots, I made up rules. I would shoot only pointed roosters. Then, only pointed roosters flushing from right to left. Finally, only pointed roosters flushing from right to left with visible spurs and a long tail. I managed to make it last one hour and a half. Thereafter, I came and paid just like any other guy. Sometimes I would bring a friend or my daughter and son. Their reaction was always equal to mine. "My Gawd! Just how many are there?"

Regent, North Dakota, had pheasants to rent, to sell, to mortgage, to give away to the poor, all because somebody decided to give nature a hand. Besides being a good guy, Lloyd Fugelstad had only one thing going for him—he was closer to Fargo. Unfortunately, he was also east of the Missouri River, and life there is hard for the ring-necked pheasant no matter what the landowner does.

Lloyd had a bright and smiling young man named Dave Carlson to help him from time to time. Among his other fine qualities, Dave had two pieces of his life that were then, and remain, inextinguishable: a love for hunting and a small, brown retriever mix that leaped all obstacles in pursuit of birds. During the hard winter of 1996 –97, Dave said flocks of pheasants gathered in feed yards, and farmers fed them. One fellow had over six hundred birds. When the winter cold and snow finally broke, he had sixty. Pheasants would simply fall over dead, exhausted from the sheer effort of staying alive. In Regent, the weather abates occasionally as the chinook winds warm the west side of North Dakota. In the east, particularly along the Missouri Coteau, there is no rest for the oppressed.

It is this part of North Dakota, the Coteau, that represents the edge of the ancient flood plain of the Missouri River. It is prairie and pothole country. In the middle of it is another oasis of man's effort to make a difference, the Lone Tree Wildlife Management Area.

When the Garrison Dam diversion became history, the land that had been acquired to hold the backwash of the defunct dam was reformed into a wildlife management area. Lying just north of Goodrich and south of Harvey, the Lone Tree contained former agricultural lands, potholes, and native prairie. Before being wiped out by the winter of 1992–'93, and again in 1996–'97, Hungarian partridges were so plentiful in the Lone Tree that a limit of huns was expected while hunting for native sharp-tailed grouse. The sharptails are still around, as they have been since the last ice age. I went there to hunt them for no better reason than the Lone Tree was close enough for me to try my hand at this new sport without putting in two days of travel.

It was there I met Scott Peterson and Terry Osbourne. Scott wears a uniform and spends most of his time at the Lone Tree headquarters as the resident game biologist. At least that was where I met with him and where he pointed out on a map of the management area where the sharptails might be. Terry and I met along a tree row. He was returning to his tractor/mower to finish a management cutting. Terry, a North Dakota farm boy complete with an old Chevy pickup and a Labrador retriever, not only pointed me in the right direction, but he helped me understand the nature and habits of the sharp-tailed grouse. There were, however, some things he didn't explain. Distance was one of them. Sharptails take a lot of walking, and when the pickup is a small, white spot on a far horizon, distance is important. Wind is another thing. The first time I stepped out of the cab of my truck, my cap was whipped from my head and into a far field. Sometimes the wind blew so hard that a flushing covey of sharptails would come to a hovering stop in midair. About the time I figured out that I didn't have to lead a standing target they would turn into the wind and be gone.

I found lodging in Goodrich and cheerfully joined the community for three or four days of the year. A hound dog could sleep in the main street of Goodrich, yet the town had a certain charm. A sign in the grocery store window stated: "Reward for the return of my extension ladder, one apple pie." I could buy a cold beer at the Goodrich Machine Co., and if I had found that extension ladder, I could have had a fine apple pie.

But there was no finer apple pie in the world than that at John's Cafe in Otterville, Missouri. The Gooseberry pie at Mary's Cafe in Prairie Home, Missouri, was pretty good too. I should know; I spent eighteen years hunting quail in Missouri. Long enough to experience the best and finally, by way of management gone bad, the bust of the quail hunting. I could have the daily special and three vegetables at a lunch room in the back of Jones' Grocery in Newark, Missouri, but, at the end, I could not have even the sight of gentleman bobwhite.

It was one of those cases where the imagination was baffled by the facts. But facts are facts, and they would not disappear because I didn't like them.

Oklahoma brought me back to quail. If Missouri was the horrible warning, then Oklahoma became the shining example. More of that later, because the fine mingling of holding on and letting go is what this book is about.

Aldo Leopold wrote, "Because everyone from Xenophon to Theodore Roosevelt said sport has value, it is assumed that this value must be indestructible." Well it's not. It takes the hand of man to keep things going. Good people can create the habitat that makes a difference. In my home state of Minnesota, right here in Cass County, I am blessed with a land department that considers its mission in timber management to be defined by the needs of our finest game bird, the ruffed grouse. What they have created and how it has worked out, thus far, have made for good stories. My friend and cattle rancher, Tom Kuschel, with the aid of a bulldozer and wandering cows, creates and maintains better habitat than the studied efforts of certain agencies. On the other hand, I don't get along with cows all that well and that too has laid the groundwork for some fine tales.

Have I taken any trophies? I have held on to and I have let go of places, people, dogs, guns, and game birds—all in pursuit of six hours of life without a care in the world. That is surely a trophy, the greatest of all and as rare as the unicorn.

Chapter One

Stirring the Mix

There is no better place for a grouse hunt than Tom Kuschel's Cow Trail cover. A square of five hundred acres, the top and right side are bordered by township roads, and the bottom and left side are framed by grass pasture. In between is a patchwork of grass openings and small, wooded islands, each one unaccountably different from the others. Along the cover's left side are two long stretches of mixed woods and poplar with a narrow trail running between them. Intersecting paths meet the trail so that deer, uneasy about the hunting dogs, can ghost away from the commotion by passing between the trees. If the light is just right, as it is when the sun is setting, the deer seem to be flowing without legs, almost sailing, their heads and necks appearing as half-furled jibs leaning from the breeze.

The Cow Trail cover is a happy accident. Cattle, aspen trees, and pasture grass have found a balance that is agreeable to ruffed grouse. Cattle are not independent thinkers; they like to follow one another. Like most herd animals, the cows stay out in the grass parts and, except for an occasional foul-tempered maverick, wander single file often enough to create paths between a supermarket of grouse food. At a distance, the Cow Trail cover looked like a wooded pasture, but up close it was grouse heaven with paths.

It seems unlikely that a cattleman could form a bird cover, but in most ways Tom got it right. The ruffed grouse requires a mix of things. In fact, the more confused, stirred up, cut down, and grown up the cover is, the better the grouse seems to like it. Which is why the bird prospers in the company of my friend Tom Kuschel and his bulldozer.

Over the years, I have found that good land like this is formed by, and forms, good people. It makes sense; there is no other material at hand. Aspen trees, like nature, abhor a vacuum. When Tom had his mature aspen cut, then bulldozed the stumps aside to make more pasture, he left the remaining trees to stand along the openings. Sometimes he windrowed the slash, pushing it into other strips of aspen. The sun warmed the soil, the aspen sprouted, and so did fruit-bearing dogwood bushes—acres of them on open edges in a profusion of plenty to the point where if they were a cash crop, Tom could have harvested them with a combine.

Tom Kuschel likes cows. To me, a cow is a snot-blowing, dog-chasing rhinoceros with a stupefied stare. A half-ton cow consumes 34,675 pounds of food and 54,750 pounds of water each year. That diet, my friends, creates a lot of manure. But it's not B.S. to Tom.

From March to May of any given year, Tom will sleep fully clothed in a recliner so that he can wake up about every four hours and help his cows have their calves. The mechanics of that process are not for the faint of heart. Contrary to Walt Disney, things do not always go smoothly—look at a device called a calf puller and you will know what I mean. Since calves equal market price, the more cynical among us would say that he is simply tending to business in order to raise his bottom line. On the other hand, when he and the few ranch hands that work with him lose only six calves in a thousand over several weeks of twenty-four-hour days, I think the bottom line shows more than the checkbook balance.

Yes, Tom really likes cows. For a time I convinced him to come with me to Missouri to hunt quail. We never turned on the radio either going down or coming back, and my view of the passing rural landscape from southern Minnesota through Iowa and into Missouri was forever altered. I don't know how much Tom got out of our trips, but I came to understand what those orderly rows of plants really were, how much they cost, how to put them in the ground, and how to take them up.

After lunch in a Missouri sales barn one particular day, Tom and our host, Dave, also a cattleman, went into the arena to watch the young stock pass through. This is what cattle guys do. I was ready to get back to bird hunting, but some things needed to be done first. The cattlemen wanted to watch the auction, therefore, so did I. There were a lot of men in cowboy hats and mud-stained jeans quietly squinting at a passing parade of young cows. Finally, I commented that the group of critters, a deceased beef-raiser's last herd, looked pretty good to me. They were sturdy, had four legs, and a fuzzy exterior.

"Pretty sad show for a lifetime of work," said Tom.

"I would have had them butchered before I sold those in public," agreed Dave. Clearly, there was more to this cattle business than met my uneducated eye. But I am capable of instruction, and another opportunity came up at the end of the day. The quail hunting was either very good, because we were done early, or it was very bad for the same reason. I don't remember. Regardless, I was in the middle of the truck seat, and it was time to feed Dave's livestock.

When I part this mortal coil, I will probably be reincarnated as a cow because I am certain our creator has a sense of humor. If that role becomes mine, I want to belong to men like Dave and Tom. I watched them during the cattle feeding and saw how they walked among the stock, how they pushed one this way and talked about another over there. Tom had traveled many hundreds of miles to hunt quail, yet he seemed more contented and at home in the middle of Dave's herd than he had been out on the cover edges. I resolved to keep my opinions of cows to myself.

If I press him hard enough, and if his chores are done, Tom Kuschel will walk with me behind the dogs. He owns better guns now, but in past years it was his habit to carry an old Model 12 Winchester with a Cutts compensator stuck on the end of its long barrel. Those devices had small tubes that screwed into the end ahead of a vented cylinder. Tom's gun had an extra-full tube cross-threaded so tightly that it had become a permanent selection. But he didn't mind. He just liked the old gun; it was lean, battered, full of memories, and, while not the most efficient at close work, it was capable of real impact when properly applied. We took a break, once, at the edge of one of the Cow Trail glades, near where the trucks were parked under some shady oaks.

I looked over at the cab of my pickup. A bee was trapped inside. Time after time he flew against the glass. He hovered up and down every square inch, confounded by the smooth, hard strength of clear air.

"I have this belief," I said, "and it's shared by a fine writer named Chris Madsen. He says that the best hunting will come to the hunter who makes the greatest effort to get it. It just seems right, you know." I waved my arm toward the Cow Trail cover. "You take this place, right now. As we lay here with the dogs, there are probably thirty grouse in five bunches within the next half mile. That sounds like heaven to me, but it all depends on your point of view."

"How so?" Tom asked.

"Two weeks ago we did that father and son thing, remember? Max and I hunted right here with you and Miles. I got a limit, and I remember Miles got four. Do you remember how many Max got?"

"Nope," answered Tom, "I just remember he missed the last one, and I missed them all."

"We probably put up twenty-five birds in two hours, just like I had hoped we would. But the last ten came up in front of Max, and he missed every one of them. If a man is what he wills himself to be, then that day I was going to be the World's Greatest Grouse Hunter. I was going to control the dogs, show everybody where to go, and ultimately bask in the full limits of a well-executed plan." I picked up a stick and pushed some leaves into a pile.

"This works, by the way, but only if you are going after sunfish, with worms, and you don't care how big the fish are."

The birds were there. I walked in on two points within the first fifty yards. Max, being a left-handed shooter, was my right-hand man. Both grouse flushed left, both died. The birds did not understand that when I walked to the left of the point it meant that the bird should go to the right. From the beginning, we had a problem with grouse comprehension and flight direction.

"Even better," I said, "the birds were in the open. The last one got caught in a grove of small aspen and was forced to hunker behind a log. It clucked a couple times to announce its departure. It was asking permission for take off," I explained to Tom.

"Only makes sense in the presence of the World's Greatest Grouse Hunter," he answered.

I pushed on. "Both dogs and birds were in front of me, and in that part of this cover things can come together like, well, sunfish and worms. But Max was still the bee at the window. I had five grouse, and he had none."

The dogs work well together, especially when they can see one another, and they go where the birds are. That turned out to be in front of Miles, Tom's son, who is the same age as Max. He didn't hit them all, but he did well enough to be four to nothing ahead of Max. This is a problem for a type-A control guy, like me. However, try as I might, the scales of justice would not even out.

"Max was firing off his shells and, except for my dark mutterings about luck, fate, and fortune, was probably having a pretty good time."

"And you hide your emotions so well," added Tom.

"You know, I can't remember if you even fired a shot," I answered.

"That's why you like to hunt with me."

"It was the last bird that I remember best. By then, I had decided to give Max shooting instructions," I continued.

"Right, being the World's Greatest Grouse Hunter and all," he said.

I dug the burnt tobacco out of my pipe with the stick. "Well, you know how it went."

Max was burned down, and the Cow Trail cover is a long circuit. By the end, we had all clumped together and were shuffling along to the trucks. I don't know which of the lesser gods is in charge of the Cow Trail. I don't think it is the Man himself, because grouse hunting and the trials of a teenaged boy are not the stuff of a vision quest. Whichever little red god it is, it has a perverse sense of humor. About twenty yards in front of the trucks, my old shorthair, Beans, locked down on a solid grouse point. The young dog occasionally makes mistakes, but the old boy is, as they say, money in the bank.

A woodcock point is kind of like a casual gesture that says, "Oh, by the way, here's something." A grouse point is an exclamation from every fiber and hair, tail tip to nose, saying, "Right here! And right now!"

Somewhere in the brain, under that lump at the back of our head, must be a marble wall in which profound images are etched forever. I can visit this monument any time I want to. The picture doesn't change, and neither do the facts.

"Max walked in with his gun up and eyes above the point, not fast, not slow, just steady. I was proud. The grouse came up, and he was a big one. A wide, gray, black-banded fan below the bright ermine specks of white against dark brown. There may have been branches in the way, and there probably was a screen of dogwood leaves." I paused, thinking back. "But to me, there was only that bird."

"Then it was gone," said Tom, after a bit.

"We could have used a replay camera," I answered. "You know what I mean. Cut! Replace the bird. Let's try that again."

"Max didn't have a problem with it," Tom answered.

"The event didn't fit my master plan," I said.

"That's what I said, Max didn't have a problem," which was followed by Tom's cracker-crunching laugh. "You need to get into cattle ranching if you want to fight real demons. I have a couple mother cows that would love to meet you when they're having a calf crossways to the chute."

"I'd rather be the benevolent god of insects," I replied. I stood up, walked over to the pickup, and opened the door. The bumblebee circled the steering wheel, banked left, and lumbered out of the opening.

"It's simpler, and the bee won't remember a thing."

Chapter Two

It Comes with Your Name

If I consider all the fine Christmas gifts that I have opened in my life, a few stand out. When I was fourteen, my Uncle Ed gave me a box of shotgun shells. Until that Christmas, our family's entire shotshell inventory consisted of Federal paper shells—the kind with roll crimps enclosing a small, circular cardboard cover stamped "#6" or "#4". They came with an unalarmed greenhead mallard printed on the boxes. Dad got two cases when he was in the state legislature in 1947, and twenty years later we were still working on the remainder. What a miracle that gift of red Super X shells appeared to be. They were smooth, bright, and welded shut. No more swelled cases. No more "poofs" from soggy powder. That same Christmas, Dad gave me twelve plastic bluebill decoys. All we had up to that point were wooden mallards—a dozen weighed more than our boat. Twice that Christmas Eve, and at least that many times the next day, I poured those shells onto the carpet and passed them between my fingers. Within three days I had found enough cord and wheel weights to rig half of the decoys.

I have three children, two girls and a boy. The eldest of the three is Tessa. She is the smiling all-American blonde on the cover of the State of Minnesota Hunting Regulations for the year 2000. The grouse she is holding in that picture is one of three that she killed that day. I had put the right gun in her hands—a lightweight Franchi 20-gauge autoloader—my English setter, Salty, was at the top of her game, and the grouse population was at its peak. In those years it was like taking a kid on a guided duck hunt in Alberta, Canada. Not much could go wrong, and success equals fun. I could have walked slower and hunted less intently, but I didn't. First, because I didn't know how; second, because she didn't require it. No quarter was asked and none was given. The problem with daughters is that they go off and find other men and another life. Now, she can't come and hunt every weekend: She married somebody like me.

Grouse hunting is probably not the first choice of kid hunting-activities. The bird is skulky and sneaky, it hangs out in dense and nasty places, and it is almost impossible to see when you finally find it. Duck hunting, on the other hand, is a lot like bluegill fishing with shotguns. When it's good, it is easy to understand. When it's bad, the decoys are still entertaining. Occasionally an otter swims by and messes with one, or an eagle might pass the blind when it checks to see if the blocks are edible. You can keep reminding your youngster that ducks fly sixty miles an hour, and that a flock might be just seconds away from pitching into the spread.

What makes the memory is the weather. We had a pothole that was a quiet harbor in the heaviest of storms; a spot where no boating was necessary. One of the hardest things about being a duck hunter is to pull yourself out from under the covers when the rain and wind are shaking the windowpanes. A promise is a promise, though, and I had promised Max that we would go, he made one to come along, so we were up.

"Only lunatics and lost dogs are out in weather like this," I said, over my coffee.

"It's okay," he responded.

Now, "It's okay" from a kid can mean anything from "I agree" when talking about how things are to "it's broken and hurts like hell" when talking about a leg.

However, getting up and dressed means the day's business was in front of us. I left the house and walked out into the wind.

Every duck hunter knows the sound. It's that first rushing noise, like an astonished crowd, when the door shuts behind you on a wind-ripped early morning. A newspaper, shiny and slick with rain, flapped across the driveway and slapped against the garage door as I raised it and walked inside. Max came across the lawn from the back door.

"We're up and dressed. What do you think? Still want to go?" I asked.

"It's okay," he answered.

It was ten miles of shiny highway and windshield wipers. The only real risk was getting wet and maybe a little cold. Nothing was freezing, the day was unique, and, best of all, we were about to separate ourselves from the ribbon clerks and become real waterfowlers, regardless of whether the ducks were flying.

Well, they weren't. But everything else was. Leaves blew past the blind in a world made horizontal by the northwest gale. Even the decoys pitched and danced. I was grateful for water that was shallow enough to let me set them with waders. The dawn came slowly; black eased into light gray and dark gray. It was just the two of us, man and boy, against the day. We couldn't talk and didn't have to. All of our senses were filled with the sound, sight, and buffeting of windblown rain. It was enough. Eventually, it was too much.

"It's 8:00 A.M., Max, and nothing's flying," I shouted. "Let's go home." He nodded, and there was a crash. A tree had blown over behind the truck and across the trail.

It was an old poplar, not real big, but more than we could drive over. We both looked at it. I thought about the tree as I picked up the blocks, hoping it would move itself out of the way.

"What do we do?" Max asked.

"It's okay," I answered. He nodded his head.

I went into the tool box for a chain and a nylon tow rope. "Loop this chain around the big end of the trunk," I said. Then I tied the tow rope to the spring shackle of the truck and to the chain on the tree.

"Stand over there while I pull the trunk to one side. Wave your hands when it's out of the way." I was not as confident as his smile.

But, it worked. We won. Twenty minutes later we were having pie and hot chocolate at the cafe.

"That was cool," he said.

Before Max was born, I heard that wind call my name one day. It was not "cool." It was as cold as death.

Lake Ada is nine hundred acres of water. Far out in the middle there is a reef of rock that rises to within a few feet of the surface. Reed cane grows there, creating an island of blowing, bending grass almost six feet high. When the diving ducks are migrating, it is the place to hide a boat. The birds feel secure so far from shore, and a J-hook of black-and-white decoys can bring them in so close that the mist blows in your face as the first ten or fifteen land and the fifty behind them stack up for their chance. The shooting is point blank.

I have a fourteen-foot aluminum boat that has been my friend and companion since I was ten years old. I picked it out myself from several that were drawn up on shore on a rainy spring day. Dad talked to the salesman, then turned to the car window and said, "Go get one." My brother, Don, and I started with a Champion two-and-a-half-horse motor that ran no more than half the time, then graduated up to and through a thirty-horsepower motor that had twice the recommended muscle. The old boat took it all and brought us home.

I could have used some of that power on Lake Ada. All I had on the transom that late afternoon was a five-and-a-half-horse Johnson.

Everything seemed so right. There was a strong wind from the northwest, spun off the face of a high-pressure center pressed up against a passing low. The perfect mix for migration. I put my dozen bluebill decoys into the boat, along with gas for the motor, a pair of oars, and a life jacket, then pushed off the trailer and into the bay. The ride out past the point got a little bouncy, but nothing that I couldn't handle with a little seamanship.

Except for my black Labrador retriever, I was alone. It was to be the last day I hunted ducks alone on big water. Looking back on it with twenty-twenty hindsight, I am stunned at my arrogance. But what could defeat me? I had a big sheepskin coat for the cold, plenty of gas, and I expected the wind to go down at sunset.

The first hint of trouble came as I tried to set decoys. I could not keep the boat in the lee of the grass island. I had set two decoys before the boat spun around in a wind gust, the propeller tied up with a decoy line, and we were adrift. I pulled up the motor as the boat skidded along the surface broadside to the waves. The line was heavy-braided nylon with a decoy on one end and a lead anchor on the other. I had no knife.

"Well, I've got a shotgun," I said to myself. I loaded the old Remington with two shells and shot the anchor end off one side of the prop and the decoy end off the other, threw the decoy into the bottom, and hit the throttle. The boat pushed against the waves and made it back to the small slick of still water along the island's lee edge.

What to do? I should have gone home, but since the wind was going to go down at sunset, and the bluebills would be pouring in, I decided that I hadn't come all the way out here for nothing. I dropped the anchor at the grass edge and played out the line as far as it would go. I set the decoys, one after the other, then pulled myself deep into the cane with the anchor rope. The sun would set in a half hour. My heavy sheepskin coat was warm and windproof, my dog was all set, and my gun was loaded.

But nothing came, except more wind. Now the cane slapped the boat, and then it laid flat. The waves would have had white caps, but the spindrift was blown off the tops. A slow, prickling surge began at my belt line, went up through my belly, then along both sides of my neck. It was real, primal fear. The light was hard and cold, and the water turned black. I was alone. No one could hear me, and in about ten minutes no one would see me.

"Time to go!" said my instincts.

"Don't panic!" my mind cautioned. "I can do this thing. Just unwind the ball piece by piece and think it through."

I dropped the anchor and tied it short, By now the waves had invaded the reed island, and the boat was bobbing in the troughs. I wasn't going to leave my decoys behind—they had been my first hunting-based Christmas present, and no lake was going to get them—so I played out the anchor line and picked them up. At first I was winding the lines in. Then I noticed that the blocks were shiny with ice. The temperature was dropping so fast that the lines began to freeze stiff. I tossed the last few decoys into the bottom of the boat. Poor old dog, hunkered in the bow; she knew, even if I hadn't figured it out.

I started the motor, left it on idle, and sat for a moment watching the bow rise and dip, tethered to the anchor and fighting the surf. I decided to go forward, pulling myself back to the reeds. When I raised the anchor, I knew that the wind would have me for the time it took to get back to the tiller handle. I was right. As soon as the bow came free, the boat surged and turned broadside, but being a fine friend, she took the first three waves without rolling. I got us turned around and back to the little bit of shelter that the island offered. There was no alternative. I had to go into the face of the beast, away from my safe harbor, and try to make the far shore.

The world becomes very small when life is the goal. All I could see was the next wave, and once over that one, the next one, and the next. When the wind blew very hard, the surface of the water was wrinkled, like a black snakeskin. I started to take spray and wave tops on board, but it didn't slosh for long—it froze on the seats and the gunnels. The decoys, bobbing around in the bottom, stopped moving and became one mass. The ice became weight, and the weight was what saved me because the little five-and-a-half-horse motor did not have enough power to hold my bow into the gale. My ship became too heavy to blow broadside, and we moved, a few feet at a time, ever closer to the leeward shore.

I made it. Idling in the dark off the lee shore of the bay, I took stock. The old coat was a solid mass on the splash side, but my steering arm was still free. There was a foot of ice inside the hull bottom, the seats and decoys were welded together, but the dog and I were alive. I pulled the gear lever back into forward and crept along the shore to the mouth of the bay, then through the gap and onto the landing.

I ran the throttle up to full speed to try for a solid beaching, but the waves had frozen into a shelf on the sand and we slid up, then back out.

Standing up, I broke my coat free of the ice holding me to the seat and stepped over the side into the water. I just had to get on dry land, and the boat was coming with me. Digging into the lake bottom and pushing hard against the stern, I made it to a crunching, sliding halt, home from the sea.

"As God is my witness," I said out loud, "I will not do that again."

I never spoke of it to anyone. Now when the wind blows sleet against my window, I go out to my little pond with its wind-sheltered, dry-land point and let it howl. That's a memory I can walk away from.

Chapter Three

Flying Liver

If woodcock tasted like grouse instead of like liver, their populations would be pressed a lot harder than they are currently. Consider that the birds lie well for a pointing dog, flush more or less straight up, and are not hard to hit. Indeed, they fill the card for all of a game bird's desirable traits—except taste. A good many young hunters and novice dogs cut their gunning teeth on woodcock, and a few old men finish their hunting careers on them. However, most every bird hunter knows that woodcock are of the strong-red-meat persuasion, and unless a man likes liver, they get waved off. A game bird ought to be lovely, and any number of wildlife prints attest to the woodcock's beauty. But you never hear of too many guys with woodcock in their game bags bragging about how good dinner is going to be. Mostly, the review revolves around the dog work, the flush, and the shot.

Woodcock are delegated to the gourmand, like many strong-tasting things, and their greatest fans are in the minority. I eat them on occasion, and I have seen other people eat them. I even saw one man eat a bird complete with entrails. That, however, was in response to a dare, and I label the act as eccentric, much the same as eating woolly worms when we were kids. For the most part, my crowd of game eaters are likely to pour Seven-Up into their red wine when it gets too strong.

I'm not accusing the serious woodcock hunter of elitism. I just question his taste buds. Does a hunter want to be well-known for seeking a bird to eat that does not have predation listed as a primary cause of decline?

I cast my vote with the predators as well as with both of my Labradors that retrieved the little fellows but always with curled lips. The woodcock is a target of opportunity that fills those hours when the grouse are in decline and the walk is long. The bird has provided distractions for bored pointing dogs and amusement for equally bored hunters.

They can be pesty. I had a grouse cover that was on the backside of a world-class woodcock thicket. There was no way to reach the grouse cover except through the middle of the buggy-whip aspen. If a hunter chose to shoot his limit of 'doodles, the grouse would be gone when he climbed out of the soft ground. Woodcock gathered in this place in such profusion that my setter would not proceed: she would not stop pointing. I had shot some of the birds in the past, and she put woodcock on her desirable list. We made a deal—I allowed her five points followed by five flushes, then I would shoot into the air. Five more points and flushes, another shot, then we were past the crowd and stepping into the grouse woods. Grouse will hold for a couple shots, as long as there isn't any shouting and whistling.

A Bird in the Hand

When every point is a multiple flush, you can't make progress. In this cover, I once put up five birds that were all in the air at the same time, and I never kicked out less than two. It was move ten feet and point, flush, then move ten more feet and point again. After my setter's seventh point, I simply picked her up and carried her through the aspen cluster, down into the creek bottom, and up the other side. If I hadn't done that we would have been forced to camp in the place and consume woodcock until they left or we quit.

I haven't seen any research on the subject, but I think that there must be an addictive juice in the fibers of red, liver-like meat. The woodcock has strong-tasting companions in the game-bird world: the snipe, the rail, the coot, even the sharp-tailed grouse. I confess to a liking for the last bird, and it may be that hunters of woodcock, or any on the list, are persuaded in the same way. I just happen to appreciate sharptails, particularly so when they are alive and under point or on the wing, quite a bit when they are in my hand, and less when they are on a plate.

Take the coot, for instance. Here is a waterbird so social that it rivals cattle in the herd mentality. Have you ever heard a duck hunter say that he accidentally shot a coot flying by itself? In my part of the flyway, we have rafts of coots—carpets of them—on the back bays and even in the open water.

I have a one-hundred-foot-long rope through which I have pushed ten fish-stringer clips, one very ten feet. I attach one blue-bill decoy on each clip, unwinding the rope as I play out the string, until the last duck in the line is clipped on.

I used the rope to finish my diver set in this fashion one late afternoon, then decided that I had earned myself a pipe. The blind was fluffed up around my boat, my faithful Labrador went on guard, and I settled in for the sunset. After a half hour, a coot flotilla paddled over to see about the new talent. As a group, they wanted to swim between the decoys on the picket line. The rope was just under the water, and when the leading coot felt the rope against its feet, it stopped. The others pressed on. In a minute or so, I had two or three thousand coots all along my decoy rope. From above, it must have looked like a football team of bluebill decoys playing in front of a stadium full of coots.

People eat coots. Some people have eaten coots without knowing what they were. By way of example, my father was in the Minnesota legislature just after World War II. He and another legislator were asked to gather enough ducks for a game dinner at which the governor and other dignitaries would be present. After the morning shoot, Dad and his partner had limits of mallard, but those weren't enough for the fifty-plus dinner guests. What to do? The coot limit was extraordinarily generous, and the chefs were very talented. Dad said, "Hell, they weren't half bad."

I have eaten them myself. I hunted with a fellow that called them "rice hens." In the course of one morning's diver hunt he killed eight. They were obliging, decoyed well, and provided work for the retriever. My partner wanted a photo of the game, so I tucked the coot heads under their wings. If the photo isn't looked at too closely, the tailgate has a fine bunch of ducks on it: bluebills, redheads, and a blue gray something every now and then. The fellow cooked them in a Crock-pot. Epicureans would say that anything cooked in a Crock-pot is edible, though often not identifiable. To which I respond, if coot is on the menu and is edible, identification is not necessary.

I eat quite a few sharptails, generally all at once over a period of five days. After my first sharptail hunt, I became more selective about the birds I ate and those I gave to landowners. My farmer hosts get the "blue backs." When I clean an old sharptail, the meat up against the backbone is a shiny bluish red color, hence the name. I'm not being mean when I give away the old birds—the landowners aren't going to eat them anyway. North Dakota farmers like beef for their red meat. I get to be a sportsman, and they get to be gracious hosts. It is a win-win situation. I'll bet that if they let me look in their freezers, I would find each year's sharptails, packaged and frozen like stone mileposts.

I like to grill the pink-meated young birds for lunch,. Sometimes I put one in a Crock-pot for dinner, or I'll cut it up and combine it with oriental fixings. But after a five-day hunt, I have had enough. No one in my home asks if I brought any sharptails back.

For quite a few seasons, several Missouri friends (more on these friends later) came north to bird hunt. Although we mainly chased grouse, Tuesday evenings were always designated as woodcock-dinner nights. One friend cooked, another cleaned the birds and kept the red wine flowing. One bottle was required for the cleaning of the woodcock; another bottle for the cooking. When a hunter has a reason to shoot them, woodcock hunting can be uncommonly fun. We were hunting the wily "mudbat" with a higher purpose, and we never lacked enough for dinner. The important ingredient in the banquet was the wine, supplemented by bourbon and beer. After a hard day in the field, backed by several mood adjusters, woodcock is edible and not identifiable. It was at this event that the woodcock with the entrails left inside was prepared and consumed. In this context, you can see how it was possible.

I have asked, but no one can find evidence of a citation issued to a hunter for having over the limit of woodcock. I count this as proof of the high moral caliber of woodcock hunters in general and of the bird's taste when eaten by those who didn't know what it was and decided to try it.

All that having been said, the woodcock is declining. Recently, a University of Minnesota research project tracing the migration patterns and travel routes of the timberdoodle fell short of funds. Within two months, Woodcock Minnesota was organized, and a group of dedicated men raised enough money to finish the compilation of data and obtain its conclusions. I joined the group. My reason was not that I loved the bird or that I wanted more of them. Rather, it was that I like the people who love the woodcock. Without the bird, we would not have come together. Hopefully, the study will indicate what needs to be done to halt the decline, because this group of men needs to gather for the same reason that the woodcock is a fine game bird. Similar to woodcock, we lie well for our pointing dogs, rise straight up when moving, and don't fly too fast; we are kind to young hunters, old bird dogs, and each other. I suspect, and I hope I never have to confirm, that we are also composed of strong, red meat.

Bob White

Chapter Four

One Bright, Shining Moment

Three drake mallards, their shining-white wing patches and green heads clear against a cloudless blue sky. From my hiding place in the frosty grass along the Saskatchewan River that was the whole picture—the three of them, well away and up in the sun.

It was still dark on the river. The morning had not yet made it above the flat line between the earth and the ducks. My Cree Indian guide and I watched them, three pairs of wings blinking back the light.

Then there were three shots, timed perfectly and deliberately, arriving at our ears after each duck was struck. Three mallard drakes in the same formation, now dead in the air and falling together. I counted time under my breath to gauge the distance. A perfect triple: three ducks, three shots, and three seconds to earth. It was then, and remains today, the best duck shooting I have ever seen.

I wanted to know who the hunter was. In my mind, I formed his image: brown-canvas clothes, a gray mustache, and sharp, bright eyes set deep in a weathered face. Perhaps he used a square-backed automatic, or at least a worn-silvered Model 12 Winchester. No camouflage for this man. He was steel and walnut. I would settle for nothing less.

I don't know what he would settle for. Maybe such shooting was routine for him. He may have been a native, like my Cree guide, firing a rusty shotgun. Whoever he was, I'm glad that I did not meet him. He was a long way off, and he needed to be. The only thing that could have diminished the wonder of that lifelong memory would have been the reality of the human that created it. Too often, we men fall short of our accomplishments.

I think great moments are best left at a distance to stand on their own merits. The real shooter and his three ducks could be in a snapshot. The man with his obvious faults, grinning and clutching the three mallards in his hand.

"That's my old man," a voice would say. "He got three ducks with three shots that day."

"Good shooting," another would answer and turn the page, the wonder of the moment lost in the album replay. But it will never be lost in my mind. The shooter rose to an immortality that will last at least for my lifetime.

Will my Cree guide remember it? I don't know; he was a stoic fellow. But I remember him. At age eighteen, he was the father of two children.

"One boy, two years old, and a little girl," he answered when I asked if he had any kids. His assets in life were a sixteen-foot aluminum boat with sofa cushions for life preservers and a twenty-five-horsepower outboard motor. He didn't need a car—there were no roads into his part of Canada—and the tribe furnished his home. Hard-faced and lean, he loved tobacco but would not drink liquor.

"Booze is for Indians. I am Cree. We never surrendered." Squinting into the raw wind with the boat at full throttle, he could light a cigarette with one match. And he could talk to the geese with his voice. They would answer with theirs, turning their heads from side to side, then dropping down to see this lonesome comrade who was singing to them.

I am not one who talks much in a blind, especially in unfamiliar territory and with a taciturn companion. My Cree guide issued simple instructions that morning.

"Don't shoot ducks until after the geese come. Don't move when they do."

That was it. The rest of the hour before sunrise was just misty breath and watching things like the three mallards and a flock of teal so large and so low that when they passed by the blind they split their combined mass into two living and flying rivers that flowed around our willow-branch walls.

I killed my first goose that morning. The Cree sang to them, and they to him. I did not look up, nor did I move until he said, "Take 'em!"

Rising from my knees, I looked up at the underbellies of the Canada geese, then shot at the white cheek-patch of the closest one. I almost lost my balance and in struggling to regain it, I had to switch to a farther target. I missed that one, too, and in despair I fired my third shot. The empty shell ejected from my pump and flipped back over my shoulder. I had blown my chance, I thought. That loose shell struck the ground behind me with a "whump" that I could feel as well as hear. Startled by the sound, I twisted around and there lay the Canada goose.

"Hmmm," said the Cree, "you got that one." His face unfolded into a grin of startlingly white teeth.

I don't think that gave him a bright, shining moment because later he told me about a hunter who brought two guns into the blind and upon rising brought six geese to earth. But I did get him to yelp in delight.

A hen mallard traced a course along the river bank. We had cleared the sky of geese, and duck shooting was open. It was my third day of the hunt, and I had cycled a lot of shells through my old Remington Model 31, enough to wear the skin off the inside knuckle of my thumb where it rested on the pistol-grip checkering. I watched the hen come, gauging the angle and distance until they looked about right. Rising up, I fired one shell. There was a lag between the report and the round balloon of feathers that floated in the air where the duck had been. Down and down she came and hit the water with a splash. I heard my guide yell from upstream: "Yeow! That's killin' 'em!" I know my three-mallard shooter was out there, but I don't think I gave him a shining moment.

The chance to go goose hunting again did not reoccur for fifteen long years. A goose was a rare prize in Minnesota when I went to Saskatchewan, but as the years passed Canada geese became more and more common around my home turf. One day my phone rang; on the other end was the only goose hunter that I knew, Jim Demgen. It was November, deer season was finished, and I had been talking to Jim about his luck at late-season diver-duck hunting. He hadn't been hunting the big water, he said, because there were geese along the Crow Wing River.

"I've spotted a big flock using a field just south of the highway. If you want to go, I'm heading out in the morning," he said. Of course I wanted to go. Jim had the equipment and the knowledge. All I had to do was show up.

I was on his doorstep at 6:00 A.M. We drove in the dark, pulling a trailer behind his Chevrolet Suburban. Jim is not a taciturn Cree. He is a hurricane of information and conversation, and the talk that morning did not stop until the truck bumped to a halt with its headlights shining across a field of cut corn. Jim bailed out and walked in the beams, looking at the ground and kicking aside crop debris.

"This is it, Teddy!" he shouted into the cab. "There's goose shit everywhere!"

The cargo doors came open, and the decoys were piled in stacks. The full body ones got the legs, and the shell decoys got the stakes. I kept them coming, while Jim set the pattern. It was still pitch-black, cold, and windy.

When we were finished with the decoys, Jim moved the truck

and trailer. I stood in the cornfield with my shotgun, a sheepskin-lined canvas coat, and a camping mattress pad. He'd be back, he said, as soon as he had the truck out of the way.

He was, and with a gesture to the left, he told me to go over to a patch of knee-high cornstalks and cover up. The geese would be along in an hour or so. I put on my canvas coat, stretched out on the mattress pad, and built a mound of cornstalks behind my head. I pulled more stalks over my body. I decided to lay on my back and look between my feet toward the decoys. My old coat has a shawl collar and that wonderful characteristic of sturdy clothes that allows you to hunker inside and peer out. The corn leaves rattled, and dark became gray dawn, which became full light. There was no honking, or any geese above me.

I looked between my feet, and in that space was a low line of dark shapes, some on each side, others coming straight in. They would flap their wings a bit, then coast, flap, and coast again. The geese had arrived without fanfare or flourish. I did not have the slightest idea of what to do next. So I did nothing.

On they came with no hesitation or flaring. When I could make out the eyes of the leader, I sat up. He sat down in the corn, and so did his flock. We all looked at one another.

He tilted his head one way, then the other way. I did not move. My gun was mounted, and my arms started to cramp. I thought about lying back down, but abandoned that idea. In the meantime, more geese came in from behind the flock walking about in front of me. They flew over the top of their grounded brothers and gave me some relief. I shot the third and fourth goose of the line. Jim finished two of his own. It was over. We met in the decoys, shook hands, and hefted our birds. They were big. They were also, Jim said, "green."

"They look okay to me."

"No, Teddy, I mean they haven't been shot at," he answered. "Let's weigh them at the country store."

The largest bird scaled in at sixteen pounds, two at fourteen, and one at twelve.

Jim and I spent the next three days hunting the fields and moving with the flock as it circulated around the area. Each day was a little harder, and on the last day we got only the powdered doughnuts I bought at the store. We had gotten so bored with waiting that we drove off for a break. Even that did not bring in the birds, but it didn't matter. An ordinary goose hunt for Jim had been one bright, shining moment for me.

I learned about geese. For instance, I learned that if I was going to continue to pick them, I would need at least five acres for the feathers. I learned that the big ones should be left to get bigger and that the young ones are much more tender. And I learned that goose hunting requires a lot of scouting and sometimes a lot of equipment.

More than all that, I learned that my mallard hunter, my Cree guide, and my goose-hunting friend were just ordinary people who came together with ordinary circumstances to create one bright, shining, extraordinary moment in my life. They didn't try to do anything special; it just turned out that way. If they had tried, none of it wouldn't have happened.

I tried. My daughter Molly was thirteen. When I was her age, I went on my first duck hunt. My dad and my brother and I traveled to a remote lake. (I could take you there today.) We all shot at one mallard duck, and I was certain that my shot, alone, had brought it down. That was the sum of our day's bag, one green-headed mallard. I thought I could do better with my child's first time. By all accounts, I did. We walked to the blind on an early morning when the day was going to dawn clear and comfortably warm. The decoys were easy to put out, and within half an hour the first duck had fallen and been retrieved by my German shorthair, Beans.

The miracle was not yet complete. In an hour, three Canada

geese passed over our blind so close that I knocked one down with duck loads. Never in all the years of our family hunts had a goose been shot .When I brought it back to the blind, I had Molly lift it and feel its weight and size.

"Well what do you think?" I asked.

"It's big," she answered.

"They used to be very rare around here," I told her. "Then, shooting a goose got you on the front-page of the paper." I was trying to draw out some sort of reaction. Something suitably awestruck.

She set down the goose and patted the dog.

Within twenty minutes I heard more geese calling, and this time ten or twelve came in for a look at the pond. One more fell.

"This is incredible, Molly, two geese in one morning!" I exclaimed.

"Yeah, okay."

It was all that; no more, no less. Looking back on it, I suppose astonishment greeted my father's first sight of an airplane. By the time I came around, planes were a common sight. For Molly, Canada geese were an everyday fixture in the water of our river home.

We forget that our shining moments have been preceded by the times and troubles that make them special. Today, a father can take a son on an elk hunt. If the father is skilled, or a guide is clever and the game is plentiful, the elk is shot dead by the boy. It's hard to convince a kid that something is a big deal when to him it hasn't been.

So, sometimes we should not try so hard. Life will sort out what defines a man's shining moment. Making it so is just ordinary people doing the ordinary things. Whether or not it shines is up to us.

Chapter Five

Neighbors, Public and Private

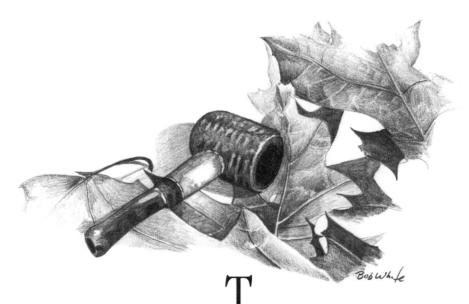

Bob White

There are always two sides to a discussion: my side, and the side no informed, well-trained, intelligent, self-respecting, sane person could possibly hold. Larry Olson is all those things, but he has the most contrary ideas about what makes good grouse cover. Larry is the wildlife technician for the Cass County Land Department. The best he can offer in support of his theories is a degree in the subject, three decades of experience in the field, and the unofficial title as the world's most effective grouse hunter. He can't have my title. First of all, I gave it to myself; second, the World's Greatest Grouse Hunter and the Perfect Dog have a lot in common—they don't exist.

The Cass County Land Department maintains, makes policy for, and plans the future of two hundred fifty thousand acres of public forest and waters. There are Balkan countries smaller than that. The department fosters the growth and welfare of over one hundred thousand acres of aspen, designing the clear-cuts into blocks of twelve to fourteen acres. Since aspen matures at forty to seventy years of age, depending upon genetics and soil composition, the work of the department is to design tree harvest around ruffed grouse. This is because all of the technicians and the land commissioner are grouse hunters. They are not Sunday walkers but are real hunters, with side-by-side doubles and (with one notable exception) pointing dogs.

In support of my side of the discussion, I have the fact that Larry Olson hunts grouse with a golden retriever. I know you are with me when I conclude that his methods must, therefore, be flawed. He follows a two-prong attack. He is of the opinion that the first year of a clear-cut is the best year.

"It's the big, green leaves of the first-year suckers," he says. "They don't frost off like everything else, and when the late afternoon of a mid-October day is sunny and quiet, the grouse are in those clear-cuts to the exclusion of everything else." Well, what can you expect from a lanky, bearded forestry type who has the appearance of an itinerant Amish gamekeeper?

Larry also supports the Fifteen Year Formula: "A clear-cut becomes perfect at fifteen years after it has been cleared, especially if it was cut in the winter."

Setting aside, for a moment, the fact that he puts more grouse in the bag than three hunters and needs a dog only to help him find dead birds, he has a terrible addiction. He loves to lay out the "long drop"; that is, he will tell a story, and you won't find out that it is a practical joke for two weeks.

We don't meet in the woods, ordinarily, because we hunt in different kinds of cover. For those of you who fish with dry flies, Larry would be a nymph fisherman. If you are a golfer, Larry would be the guy that hits them down the middle and stays in the fairway. I spend all my time in the rough, looking for my ball. That's why I have pointing dogs. We met in the woods one time, to the stunned and delighted surprise of both of us, but the meeting was preordained by the close connection of two productive covers, one on public land and one private.

It all started because desperate times—meaning a down year—require desperate measures. In down years, I always say, there are as many grouse as ever, they are just farther apart. Well, this had become one of those years where "farther" was measured in miles. I had run out of ideas. My hunting partner, Bill Habein, had run out of them as well. It was late afternoon, and in spite of the pretty leaves and the joy of just being outdoors, the topic had turned to the reality that we were birdless.

"You can bet Larry Olson isn't having this luck," I said.

"Did you ask him?" answered Bill.

"Hell no! I'm not going to give him the satisfaction of hearing me whine," I said. Besides, he'd probably tell me to hunt the green, leafy clear-cuts."

"You mean like that one over there," he said, and pointed his pipe stem at an opening absolutely glowing with vibrant green.

I looked, poked at the dirt with a stick, and looked again. "You don't suppose?"

Bill stood up, slung on his vest, and said, "What's that you always say? 'No guts, no air medal.'"

We crossed the fence from our private holding and walked down the tote trail to where it entered a square of aspen whips, each one holding three or four big, green leaves. In the center was a brush pile.

"I'll walk right at the pile," I said.

"I'll walk on your right," replied Bill. He set off with his springer spaniel, boring through the hip-high brush like a shark after herring.

My English setter, Salty, was with me that day, accompanied by Jet, her loyal black Labrador retriever and servant. True to the season, nothing happened. I stood at the brush pile for a moment—birdless as before—then Salty locked on point, solid at the base of the pile.

"Point!" I yelled. This sparked the first flush, right to left, out of the green leaves. The bird fell dead at the shot.

"Bird's up!" Bill yelled and killed another over on his side. His shot flushed a second grouse holding tight under Salty's nose, and while Jet was coming back with my first bird, the second fell almost on top of her. I opened the double—my old Parker extractor gun—spinning it in my hands to throw out the empties. A third grouse flushed straightaway, and I heard a shot from Bill's side. There was no time to look. I had shut the gun and walked to the left when a final grouse came up at my feet and died for its tardiness.

Four birds up and three down on my side of the pile; two up and two down on Bill's side. We stood grinning at each other.

"My lips are sealed," I hollered to him.

"A gift from the government," he answered.

In the words of former UCLA basketball coach John Wooden, it's what you learn after you know it all that counts. There might be something to this public management after all.

A few lean years followed that day, Salty and Jet finished their careers, and my friend Tom Kuschel acquired a holding of mixed hardwood and grassland bordering a large tract of Cass County public land. He clear-cut the aspen, leaving large islands of oak and younger trees. The stumps were bulldozed into the island edges, and the clearings seeded with a grass and clover mix. The public land right across the fence had been clear-cut in Larry's trademark checkerboard pattern, but many years ago. Fifteen years ago to be exact.

Tom Kuschel's pasture land became my Oakey Ground cover. It was then, and still is, a haven for ruffed grouse. Compared to the adjoining public land, it is a supermarket of clover greens and berries. It is not uncommon to find birds in certain locations time after time. Given the unsportsmanlike conduct of ruffed grouse in general and of specific birds in particular, the grouse here can throw down personal challenges.

Take, for instance, the brown-tailed female that took up residence in the little triangle close to the swamp. I overlooked this place until my shorthair, Beans, swung wide on our walk back to the third island. I held up for a bit and watched him. In circumstances like this, a pointing dog is a benefit to the foot hunter because you can save some steps by letting the dog check odd corners. He found the grouse far out on the edge. She spooked early, apparently aware of her exposed hiding place, and flew into the heavier trees. It was an easy mark, and both of my shorthairs, Beans and Butch, were on the trail. They found her quickly and pointed. I walked in, confident of an easy opportunity. When she flushed, my first shot struck a tree that she ducked behind, and my second went right as she juked left.

"No matter," I muttered. "I saw where she landed. Hunt 'em up, boys."

The second flush off another double point was a rising shot that I missed in front because she treed. Then, I missed above because she dove out of the tree and went low, cutting left and right between the oaks.

"I've got her now," I growled. "She cut back the way we came."

By this time I had identified her as female from the interrupted band on her brown tail. I thought she was very cagey for a bird with a brain the size of a pea. We arrived at the only spot left where she could be. After five minutes of poking and puffing, I came to a halt. Except for the places that we had already been, I could look clear through the little corner. There was no place left to hide. Therefore, she must be here. Naturally, we never found her.

I don't return to a cover very often. The Oakey Ground usually gets two visits a year, but I made an exception for the brown female and came back a third time. We went directly to the little triangle. The dogs swept through the open parts without success.

Thinking out loud, I muttered, "I wonder if she's not at home?"

I called the dogs, gesturing for a left-hand sweep.

"Yes I am!" she answered with a thundering wing-roar and, rising from behind me, zipped over my head and flew straightaway into the dense part of the corner. I executed a perfect spin, lost my cap, and took an off-balance poke.

There was a ripple of scattered applause and laughing. My sidetrip to the corner cover had been in full view of my three companions. We had finished hunting the Oakey Ground, and instead of taking a break with my partners, I paused, then announced that the nondescript little corner appeared to me to be the sort of place where a grouse might hide. Well, I thought, if I can't be a good example, then I'll have to be a horrible warning. I walked back to the group.

We were four men and seven dogs. Spence Turner, my vertically challenged Missouri import, had two setters, both wearing a beeper collar. Joel Vance, the Cisco Kid to Spence's Pancho, had two Brittanies and a beeper to go with each. Bill Habein had his springer with no beeper. That was just as well because if the dog had been wearing one we would have experienced beeper noise with a Doppler effect.

I opened my folding knife and drew the four corners of the Oakey Ground into the mud bottom of a dry puddle. Then, I added the shape of the adjoining county land. We were in the lower right corner of the county land on a fence line that separated the two holdings.

"Here's what we will do," I said. "Do you see how the swamp on the left is broad over here?" I asked, tapping a point about midway along the bottom of the county ground.

They nodded.

"This bottom line is a road. The swamp narrows at the top where it meets the road we drove in on, up there, a mile away. The fence is on our right, the swamp is on our left. We'll spread out on the base, here and here and here," I said, making little holes where each hunter would start. "Then we'll work north and easterly, with beepers in the middle and quiet guys on the outside, ending up at the narrow end." I took the swamp side. Bill had the fence line.

"Take no prisoners," I added, "and bayonet the wounded." It was going to be great.

This was not going to be a walk in the park, I thought, as we passed through the roadside barrier of sun-flourishing brush and debris. Within twenty yards, I realized how wrong I was. At fifteen years old, aspen regrowth is a park. My experience with aspen covers up to that moment had been consistent with the statistical norm of thirty thousand stems per acre—covers so thick that you can't fall down in them. Suddenly, I thought I was in Europe. After fifteen years, the trees had sorted themselves into an orderly, if haphazard, presentation. We were advancing like soldiers through the peach orchards of Shiloh. True, it was more like a line of soldiers preceded by the sound of several front-end loaders backing up, but it was not difficult at all.

"This is going to be a walk in the woods," I muttered, and started thinking black thoughts about Larry Olson's long drop.

Looking back on it, now, I like to think that all the grouse raised on Tom's side in the Oakey Ground had been chased into the aspen. I like to think that, but it doesn't compute. There were grouse to spare, and the little red gods know we spared quite a few. Larry was right. The birds are in those places.

Not only was Larry right, but, magically, there he was in person.

The rank passed on by, firing and beeping and yelling.

"My hunting partner is out there some place," he said.

"I hope he hides behind a tree," I answered.

Larry and his buddy had come in from the public side, crossed the swamp, and entered my line of march. There was only one thing for me to do. I opened my gun, then dug out my pipe and lit it.

A setter swept by, checked out the golden retriever for a moment, and charged on its beeping way toward a shot.

Larry rubbed his chin, "I thought maybe the loggers came back," he said.

"I thought you were pulling my leg about these old clear-cuts," I said. "Is it always like this?"

His eyes danced, and he grinned as he shut his 20 gauge. "You'll never know for sure."

Then he drifted off between the trees. I continued north in pursuit of the lost battalion.

Success eludes me. Although I can't remember whether we did well or just made noise, I do recall one thing. We were all on the road, dusting off, gathering dogs, and trading stories when a flock of wood ducks lifted from a nearby ditch. Of course, being a loyal and law-abiding citizen, I immediately switched my upland loads to nontoxic shot. Among the rising, circus-wagon-colored curtain was a spectacular drake. My little 20-gauge Westley Richards is lethal for all winged fowl within twenty-five yards, and that beautiful drake fell across the ditch. I didn't know if my shorthair Beans would cross water, find the bird, and return without leaving it on the other side.

I sent him, and he came back. The duck is on my mantel, permanently crouched on a limb. A symbol, in a way, of how a curious mix of private ways and public methods can produce some beautiful and unpredictable results.

Bob White

Chapter Six

Public Works

The taxpayers let go, and the county hung on. In the process, called tax forfeiture, my home county gained two hundred fifty thousand acres of buckbrush and deer flies. Cass County is mostly sand and rock mixed with a clay binder where it will vex farmers the most. It was hard country when the government was giving it away to the railroad and the timber companies, and it never changed. An anything-for-a-buck philosophy passed the tree-stump land to the timber company's realtors. The Immigration Land Company flourished, selling acreage to the settlers that followed the tracks to the northland. Not many stayed. Their expectations far exceeded the dream-bearing capacity of the land.

It was the classic immigrant tale told over and over. Ole is on the boat as it enters New York harbor. Overcome by the grandeur of the city landscape, he holds up a handful of letters.

"Yu see dees, Sven?" he said. "All of dem tell vhat a fine place I am going to!"

"Yah sure," says Sven.

"Dis ist my cusin, Einer, dah land seller!"

"Yah sure," answers Sven.

"Und if New York ist dis nice, yust tink how nice it tis in Backus!"

From time to time, county land was sold to taxpayers at low prices just to get it back on the tax rolls. No one wanted the regrowth aspen, the swampy potholes, or the rock ridges. All the big pine was gone, and nothing but "weed trees" had sprung back into the sun. The aspen had arrived. It cured like fine wine until the current class of foresters arrived. At the same time, the wood-products industry developed the concept of fiber for paper and warpless, grainless, super-strong, glue-based boards and beams.

At exactly the right time, Cass County, the Cass County Land Department, and land management came together. Aspen became a cash crop, rising from $5 per cord to $55 per cord. The county made money with land management, and the land commissioner showed them how to do it—with a twist. In Cass County, the land commissioner was Norm Moody, an English setter owner with a passion for grouse hunting. Since he already had Larry Olson in the department, every falling tree took a ruffed grouse spin. The disciples of renown grouse researcher Gordon Gullion had arrived and were out there on the ground designing bird habitat.

Those old tax-forfeit farms didn't all die out. Some were turned into new operations. A lot of Tom Kuschel's country was once tax-forfeit land, but a cattle rancher is not in the business of wood harvesting or wildlife-habitat design. Grouse covers just happen when vegetation goes down and grows back. The "County Boys" did it on purpose. Some of it was land planning, and some was skillful neglect. In every case, as I see it, they were pushing that fifteen-year window across the aerial photos. As an added bonus, if a bird-hunting land technician's career lasted long enough, he could come up with a new bunch of grouse covers every year.

The Wagon Wheel was a classic example of skillful neglect. It was half swamp and alders, with a border of mature aspen backed by a hay field and fronted by a highway. Woodcock loved it; therefore, everything else hated it—with one exception. There was a certain Missouri-bred, bandy-legged, tight-wired bundle of bird hunter named Joel Vance. He went over his boots in the acid-brown waters of the Wagon Wheel on his first day in it and became the bridge troll of the place ever after. No man, or beast, knew it better. Do you remember that movie about the Iowa farmer who built a baseball diamond in a cornfield? Every day the diamond swallowed up the spirits of long-gone baseball players and brought them back to play the next day. Well, that was Vance and the Wagon Wheel. I saw him do it. He could step into the alders and be gone.

It is said that a common man can walk on water if he knows where the rocks are. Vance knew, and he punctuated his walking and dog work with a chorus of shouts, shots, curses, and encouragement. The woodcock paid the price of landing in a narrow corner. The grouse were more tactical. They could be found right along the edge of the swamp, or along the edge of the hay field. Generally they lived among the aspen trees in a narrow belt between the brown-water sink holes and the hay rake. When he was finished with the woodcock, Joel would cross the soft ground and join us near the field.

Then two things happened: the hay field was sold for a mobile-home site, and the county sold the aspen for cutting. I went back into the Wagon Wheel this year. It is still county land, and the alder bog is unchanged. I even put up four grouse, but they were all on the edge of a mobile home's lawn. I can't fault the timber sale— the aspen was getting old enough for the trees to grow mushrooms. But a grouse is hard enough to hit without worrying about stray pellets rattling a tin-sided box. I let go of the Wagon Wheel.

If a hunter could rise high enough into the air and hover above the Wagon Wheel, to the north he would see the Bull Moose Wildlife Management Area. Before it was fully "civilized," by way of a title and a combination of county and state funds, the land was, truly, six miles of bad road and the overgrown remnants of three or four old farmsteads laid out along the South Fork of the Pine River.

The road was so bad that there was a rumor, an item of folklore, surrounding a road grader alleged to be submerged in the middle of the softest section. I always put that story with the one or two others about a train or a horse and wagon at the bottom of various bog lakes. Such tales were usually connected with a beer-breathed whisper about the dangers of travel over ice. I liked the road-grader tale.

I can say from personal experience that if a metal detector is ever used to find the grader, it will ring a positive when it passes over a hubcap from my Toyota Corolla wagon. I barely made it out one soft-mud day, and I did not go back to look for the wheel cover. It all came from my passion, at that time, to hunt ducks in remote places. The Bull Moose was so remote that daybreak there came a half hour later than normal. The little Toyota wagon had a narrow wheelbase, so I could drive with one side on the edge of the road and the other two wheels in the grassy middle. However, the car could not swim. I had to pull up short of the man-made dam by about a half mile.

Within a year of its construction, beaver had filled the spillway of the dam with mud and brush. The size of the impoundment tripled, and water ran out of the ends of the dam and into the woods, flowing down the road until stopped by the rise of a pine ridge. It added to the mystery of an early morning. I have never been to the Everglades, but I thought about it every time I loaded my decoys and gear into a little, wooden pirogue, then pulled it down the middle of the flooded road in the moonlight.

It was about another quarter mile to a small, round-topped hill. Pulling the boat up and over the hill returned me to the water, then it was a short haul to the earth berm where my Labrador retriever and I would rest for a bit, shake out the blocks into the bottom of the boat and push off. The impoundment had flooded timber, grassy islands, and everything else duck habitat could hold. I had some hunting success there, and even more success beating the odds against survival. Not everyone was so lucky.

There was nothing fatal you understand, at least nothing fatal to humans. For some people, a flooded road is nothing more than an invitation to test the off-road capability of their four-wheel drive. That is what was written on the side of the small truck I waded past. It was sitting in a hole, tipped forward, with the hood propped open. I looked in at the motor. It lay against the far fender, resting and quiet. Underneath, the blunt end of a rock had lifted the engine off its mounts.

"Gee, what a shame, Dixie," I said to my retriever. "It's gut shot and dead."

There was a second, full-sized Ford pickup at the dam. Hunkered inside were four young fellows waiting for the sun to rise on their new day. I waved, set my pirogue in the water, and paddled off. I wondered whether the next folklore story would be about a small truck at the bottom of a certain hole in the road, because the fellows in the Ford would have to drive over the top of it to get back out.

Before county officials got into the dam-building business, they planned and sold a group of clear-cuts downriver. Three hills dominate the low ground. On the crest of the largest hill are a grove of apple trees and a long line of willows. Here and there is a fence post, a yard opening, and a general orientation to the upriver side that faces the east-to-west course of Cedar Creek. When the water came up, so did the level of the creek; thus, the three hills became isolated from the log-hauling roads to the south. That's how the ground laid out from the pine ridge, where I parked to go duck hunting, down to the highway bordering the Wagon Wheel.

At around 8 A.M., all the ducks that were going to fly into or out of the Bull Moose impoundment had done so. The tug back to the car always seemed twice as long. It took about an hour, with stops to rest and sometimes to shoot at grouse with high-base duck loads. I don't remember getting grouse, but I am sure I never wounded the ones I hit. The hip boots and heavy clothes ended up in the back of the car, and my English setter, 20-gauge bird gun, and walking boots came out. My black Labrador was the cement that held the whole adventure together, so she joined in, and we three walked through the pines to the top of a ridge. This would have been the field edge of someone's tax-forfeited farm, but now it grew stunted jack pine and hazel brush right down to the edge of Cedar Creek. Years before, the first settlers laid up an earthen berm across the creek. The bridge was long gone, and in its place were two birch logs, side by side, above six feet of air and four feet of water.

Every trip across the creek was a test of faith. Would the birch trunks hold? I didn't put them there, the Stigman boys did. I found the crossing because I could see the square of a clear-cut on the hill face and wanted to hunt it. I got across on my first try, but after that it was a toss of the dice with the same odds every time. I found the three Stigmans—father and two sons—duck hunting along a beaver dam on the far side of the hill.

They were surprised to meet another hunter and pleased that, given my upland garb, I was not going to be a threat to their waterfowling.

"We never see anybody back here," said father Stigman, and his boys nodded their heads. "That's why we like it."

I left them to tend their decoys. Old Model 12 Winchester shot-guns, a battered Browning square-back automatic, and faded canvas jackets testified to an easy competence in the trade. I must have left them with the same impression, because three weeks later the elder Stigman stopped by my law office. He reached in his pocket and took out a blackened corncob pipe.

"I figured this was yours. My boy found it next to a log on the far side of the big hill." He placed my favorite hunting pipe on my desk's glass top.

"How did you know it was mine?" I asked.

"It was way back where no one else goes. When we talked, you smelled like pipe tobacco." He smiled, I thanked him, and he walked out. I never saw him or his boys again. I'll bet a lot of ducks and deer had the same experience.

A few years passed. The grouse cycle went down, and I started to search out old haunts. The Bull Moose came to mind, and with a couple false starts caused by the civilized nature of the roads and clearings, I found what looked to be my old parking area on the pine ridge. The shorthairs came out of the back of my white Ford pickup, the 20 gauge got loaded, and we were on our way to renew the old in new and exciting ways.

I was right, at least about the added stimulation. I could not find the old crossing due to the number of all-terrain-vehicle trails pounded into the field grass. I followed one trail to Cedar Creek, where there was a muddy mess into and out of the water. It was too high for my boots, so I turned to go, slipped, and fell into the creek. It was one of those ice-cold-water-sloshing-in-the-boots kind of falls. I thought about going farther, but my birch-trunk bridge was gone.

"That's it boys," I mumbled. "This place has gone to the road warriors."

I decided to cut the walk as short as possible. There were a number of trails, but I forgot to figure in the nature of the ATV user: When you have all the gas and power in the world, it doesn't make any difference where you go.

I wandered, like Moses in the wilderness, and lost my orientation. It was on par with getting pecked to death by ducks. Every trail led to another one. Even worse, I saw another pickup, a white one. Someone else was in here, and he had a truck just like mine.

"You bloody fool," I said aloud. "It's yours."

I like the thought that my taxes help pay the salary of bird-cover designers. Setting aside that Larry Olson, Norm Moody, every land department technician, and I share a common bond, it is a policy in my neighborhood to help make more wild birds, and among them is my favorite—the ruffed grouse. My problem is that I want all of the other taxpayers who don't hunt grouse to go away.

It's not like the off-road ATV users crowd in on me. I try to keep apart from them and the areas that they use. It's the marks they leave behind that trouble me. What is that statement about mountains? We climb them because they are there. Guess what? Some of us go around them for the very same reason.

Public land for parks and stadiums and race tracks, yes; but out here among the buckbrush and deer flies, public places need more privacy.

Chapter Seven

It's a Long Road

I saw the drop of water fall from the brim of my hat. It twinkled once in the sun, then spattered in the dust. More dust puffed between the cleats of my boot soles as I picked up each foot, then brought it down. Another drop formed on the edge of my hat brim and followed the line of the first, striking the trail a little farther on.

"That's sweat," I said to myself. "I've soaked through my shirt and my cap, and I've got another four hundred yards to the truck. I'm so tired that I can't lift my head to look where I'm going."

Not that it made any difference at that time of the day, but my State Trail cover was one way down and, therefore, the same way back. Two and a half miles in each direction, and without great expectations for the return trip.

A lot of bad jokes have been made about George Custer's last thoughts at the battle of the Little Big Horn. My favorite is: "Well, at least we don't have to go back across South Dakota." When the grouse hunting is bad along the State Trail, I think about George and other roads.

This cover starts at the edge of the last pasture in Tom Kuschel's country. It is a southbound pathway connecting one county-managed clear-cut after another and is the main trunk road in the tree-harvest system for a big piece of public land. When the birds are in the cuts and the flush rate is high, the best part is anticipating the return trip. On this day, however, there was not even a sound flush.

The dogs are always enthusiastic on the way down, diving into the side covers and working the edges of the regrowth portions. On the way back, there is no fooling them. They have their old and unsuccessful tracks to follow, the same as me.

I had one more low area to wade across, then a hill to climb, and the fence next to the final clear-cut would be in sight. The last of my energy was spent balancing on the grass humps waving my arms and lifting my legs like a demented crane. We were a sad-looking lot that crossed the fence and shuffled to the truck.

A beer for me, water for the dogs, then a spot in the shade collapsed into a canvas chair. The sunset would be beautiful; a good time to reflect on past sins and good days, like the time a doe and two fawns walked right past me during a lunch break in this very spot. You never know what will happen on the State Trail or, for that matter, on any road that you set out upon.

One morning it begins quickly. Five grouse feeding under the jack pines within thirty yards of the truck. In a moment, the dogs go from full charge to a hit-the-brakes point to a double retrieve. I follow them along the swamp edge and collect one more bird. Three grouse in the game bag, and the sun is still pinking the tree tops. On another morning it is just a stroll.

The clear-cut squares share the road as a common boundary, but the parcel is so large that a foot hunter must cover ground quickly. He must use his dogs like a fisherman uses a fish finder to search a big lake. The first bird will tell me everything I need to know, but I need to get him. Even a point will help. Once that first productive point happens, I can predict with some certainty where to go for another. If I kill the bird, I can open the crop and examine the contents. Trout fishermen try to match the hatch. I can look at the leaves and cuttings in the crop and tell you where the next bird is going to be. I have also found some surprises in grouse crops: a six-inch garter snake, a frog, grasshoppers, poisonous mushrooms, and, once, a small mouse. Setting aside the eccentrics in the grouse population, the crop content is my map. However, if the day is against me, and no bird comes to hand, I am strolling with the gun and trolling with my dogs.

A private holding such as an old farm or a small woodlot imposes some limits on the birds. I can organize a hunt by intersecting trails or islands of gray dogwood. A big piece of state land requires aerial photography. A five-by-seven-inch print can lift you above the trees and show you where the next cut is located. If you know how to read the infrared colors, the aspen groves are displayed as well. The County Boys have the aerial photos, and I have had some good-humored discussions with them about how the shots of the fifteen-year-old clear-cuts seem to be missing from their photo collection. In response they were kind enough to offer an eight-by-ten-inch color print of a favorite cover of mine at a silent auction to benefit our upland bird camp for kids—a charitable activity of our local Deep Portage Ruffed Grouse Society chapter. Needless to say, I bought the print but only after some spirited bidding. I have not returned to the subject of aerial photographs with the County Boys.

But I did return to the State Trail after a snowfall. I haven't figured out what to do when snow blankets my grouse covers. If it comes too early, I haven't reached that state of "good tired," and I am not ready to quit for the year. All the leaves have fallen, and a gray-and-brown shorthair does not disappear within the first fifty feet of a brushy corner. As long as the woods stay open, opportunities for finding and shooting grouse are weighted heavily in favor of the hunter who puts on an extra shirt and switches to a tighter choke. The grouse smorgasbord is reduced to whatever is green, which narrows their feeding options considerably. It is not a surprise to me when deer hunters are full of reports of the multiple birds they have seen. Setting aside the tall tales of grouse shot from trees like Christmas ornaments, a November hunt has good things for someone willing to put in the miles. Once the snow comes, however, they have me as crossed up as they do in the early season. In September, they are everywhere feeding on everything. In November, with snow on the ground, they are nowhere. At least nowhere I seem to go.

Tom had told me about the birds that his deer hunters had seen on the State Trail. I saw this as an omen for a productive day, and taking the cue, I pulled my son, Max, from his Sunday plans. We would wade the eight inches of snow. That many grouse had to be a deer-hunter fiction, but half that many would be sufficient.

It was overcast and gray. There was a pickup and trailer parked in the pasture, and all-terrain-vehicle tracks led off to the State Trail. No matter—we would walk on another part and concentrate our hunt in the areas where the ATVs couldn't go. The best effort should equal the best result. We followed Beans into the young aspen, skirting each opening and picking along the edges. Snow covers up a lot of foot catchers, and we stumbled more than we walked. Three hours of effort produced two flushes. Both birds were buried in lose snow and let the dog and the two of us walk by, bursting out behind us. It was hard hunting, and we returned to the truck tired and birdless.

I called Tom the next day to see if we had been in the right spot.

"Well, it sounds like it," he said.

"I saw a truck and a small trailer in the pasture," I replied. "Do you have someone taking down deer stands in the state piece?"

"No," he said, "that was two of our deer hunters. They came back with ATVs and drove the trail. They got nine birds. Shot them right off the trail and out of the trees."

"Max and I put up only two," I said, "and we busted our tail for those."

"I think the sound of a motor hypnotizes them, Ted. These guys are not bird hunters. They said they never left their seats. They just shot the birds and scooped them up."

Not exactly the greatest effort, but it was consistent with the grand tradition of road hunting. I did some in my early days, especially with my dad and brother. Grouse were a bonus for driving the jeep in thick places, something my dad liked to do. The practice had been modernized.

It never ceases to amaze me to learn what certain people will do to avoid a short walk along a public road. However, the practice turned out badly for one carload of road hunters. I must not have been the only bird hunter annoyed by the grouse murder. Enough of my colleagues complained, so state enforcement officers set up a grouse decoy and a video camera in the grass on the side of a trail. A car came along (they have this on tape) with the window rolled down. The passenger spotted the decoy, slid his gun out of the window, and shot the stuffed bird. The conservation officer stepped from his blind and pulled the door open announcing that the passenger was under arrest. Two things happened: the guy jerked and shot a hole in the floor of the car, then his dog jumped out of the back seat, trotted down the road, and retrieved the decoy.

"We are going to designate this a Hunter Walking Trail," Norm Moody told me. "We block the road entrance and place signs indicating that ATVs and any other form of motor vehicle are not allowed on county-managed land."

"A sign is an invitation and a challenge, Norm. It's like having a pet turtle that spends all day trying to figure out how to get around the gate."

Norm and I were on a snow hunt. He had listened patiently to my whining about ATVs overruning the land and grouse leaving for warm places when the flakes piled up, then invited me to go with him and his setters to a public area developed by the department.

"We have highland and lowland cuts in three types of habitat. All of it is tied together with a walking trail." He was optimistic.

He stopped his van at the parking area. Of course, the first thing we saw was a set of ATV tracks climbing over the earth berm and going around the gate.

"Probably a guy that decided the red circle and slash across the ATV logo did not bar his particular brand," I speculated.

"He better keep moving," said Norm darkly but undeterred.

The guy didn't get all of the grouse. In fact, I didn't see evidence that he got any. It was a day when the few birds we had chances at were holding for a point. I remember that Norm got one. I had a chance at an incoming flush but missed, as I usually do on those types of shots. More than that, I remember that we made a good effort and were rewarded with the best hunting; not of the season, but for that day.

This long road turned into a campfire. Norm had carried two cans of Coca-Cola wrapped in newspaper. He used the newspaper to start a fire, then we roasted two bratwurst and drank the Cokes. Unfortunately, it was too cold to take a nap. Norm likes naps: I think he and his two setters can curl up (after walking around in a circle two or three times) and nap almost on cue. I just hope he and his dogs stay off those walking trails because the chances of getting run over by an ATV are still pretty good.

Chapter Eight

Trading Places

Barter: To exchange by trade one thing for another. Being an attorney by profession, I add three more words to this definition: "of equal value." That should make everybody happy, unless the "trade" involves a divorce settlement. In that case, the perfect barter is when one side feels they gave too much, and the other side feels they didn't get enough, because, as Mark Twain said, "Every pancake, no matter how thin, has two sides."

For eighteen years I traded grouse hunting for quail hunting. I wasn't always so passionate about ruffed grouse. Hunting the bird on its terms, on my feet, without the aide of a running motor and a roadside is a complex pastime. Grouse don't hang out in cornfields or open expanses of foxtail weed. I heard one of my Missouri friends describe his first grouse hunt: "How duz it work? Waal, ya fill a draw full of brush, th'ow in a big quail, and dive in after it."

My stock in the grouse-hunting trade is a string of pearls—one cover after another, all connected by landowner permission and hard-won experience. Indeed, my pearls are not those of personal adornment but of individual, perfect, private, and productive grouse covers. A collection, if you will, of places I had uncovered where grouse were found in numbers that would stagger the imagination of eastern hunters. When a good day came together, I could expect to exceed fifty flushes a day.

My quail hunting friends—three of them—came from Missouri. All of them had double guns, all had pointing dogs. Two were outdoor writers working for the state of Missouri, and the third was the state trout biologist. They came to Minnesota to hunt ruffed grouse, and who better to hunt with, said their contact, than me. With the hindsight of years their opinions are probably different now, but they would all agree on one thing: their lanky host with the Labrador retriever was consumed with the passion called grouse hunting. One of them gave me the highest compliment I could receive. As he pulled off his boots and laid back in the car seat, he muttered, "Lawd, he like to have killed me!"

Joel Vance is the first of the three that comes to mind. I was in the waiting room of our local clinic and had picked up an outdoor magazine. One of the articles was a collection of dog stories; not I-had-a-dog-and-it-died tales, but incidents with retrieving mishaps, chicken killing, and all of the things that dogs get their hunters into. At first I chuckled quietly, then laughed, and finally, when I hit the one about the black Lab and the chickens, I could not hold it in. I laughed so hard, publicly and openly, that I fell off the chair. Tears ran from my eyes. That is a writer's gift to the world. Joel Vance wrote that article.

He is a steel-sprung sort of guy. A small, fast roadster with a big V-8 engine. Sometimes when he got in a curve he would go straight off the road, but he was never dull company. In our years together, I saw him fall into the worse shooting slumps I have ever witnessed. Then, he would turn right around and make an impossible shot. He loved Britannies. The one he had with him at our first meeting was Ginger. She was then, and remains in my mind today, the fastest animal I have ever seen cover ground. That does not say how fast she really was, but I owned an English setter that stood tall and bony and could cover a cornfield so fast that her body striking the stalks sounded like an artillery shell passing through trees. Ginger would have lapped that dog at least once on any race track. She did not make many grouse points, which is just as well. If she had hit a point at her usual speed, the energy she created in her slipstream would have shot past and killed the bird. Joel was also the worst off-road driver I have met. Patience was not in him. A mud hole was just an opportunity to find bottom. He once buried his long-suffering front-wheel-drive car in a bad piece of road. No amount of digging and shoulder-to-the-fender effort would get it out. So he left us and returned with a neighboring farmer and a four-wheel-drive truck. Did he talk about the pedal-to-the-metal process that got him in the mud? No, he was excited by the flock of snipe that he saw in the farmer's flooded field.

Spence Turner was the trout biologist and a vertically challenged, pear-shaped student of dogs, fish, and fly rods. Spence did not walk through heavy cover, he rolled through it like a tank. I never weighed it, but I suspect that his bird-hunting vest was at least fifty pounds. Nothing except shotgun shells ever came out of it once the item went in. Spence loved English setters. The first point I ever saw was by a Turner setter. It seems strange to say it now, but I had no idea why the dog had stopped. I thought it wanted to rest, so I sat down on a log with my Lab beside me. What could be more nostalgic? A hunter and his dog in a yellow-leafed glade of aspen.

"Point!" Spence hollered as he came rolling up.

"Point at what?" I asked.

"No, no, the dog," he said and gestured toward his setter. "The dog has a point."

"Well," I said, trying to humor this newly met companion, "what point is she trying to make?"

"Dammit! There's a bird there."

I glanced over at the clump of brush. "Nah, she's just resting."

Spence gestured again, impatient with such obtuse ignorance. I can still see the small fingers on his left hand, bright white in a golf glove. "Just stay there."

He walked in, the bird flew up, and it died. His fifth of the day.

"I'll be damned," I said. "I had no idea. Do they do that all the time?" I had become a convert in a single, shining moment.

Mike McIntosh was, then, pretty much what he is today; a modern version of the Confederate general James Longstreet. You need to find an old tintype to prove my point, but trust me, the similarities are startling. He approached bird hunting, writing, and life in the same manner—calculate the objective, determine the facts, gather the two together, then act. He was a fine figure of a man and suitable for any outdoor catalog cover. Moreover, he knew fine bird guns, owned several, and started me on the road to finding one for myself. Mike had one disturbing trait. He kept himself so open to new terrain that it was not unusual for him to wander off to investigate a field edge for arrow heads or a clump of berry bushes just to see why they were so red.

Grouse hunting is best done with one other person, equally skilled, that keeps pace with his companion. It is a complex process to keep track of three other guys and up to five dogs in a dense chunk of woods. We stirred up a lot of birds, though, and to paraphrase a line from a John Wayne movie, we had guns (and dogs) and were willing to use them.

As the years went by, the Missouri boys would bring people with them. Andy Vance, Joel's son, came complete with his own Britanny. Andy was a bird hunter, a walking grouse hawk. He suffered no nonsense from his dog nor from the birds. Dave Mackey was a classic Missouri good old boy. He carried a 20-gauge Winchester pump, and after the first day of "diving in after 'em," killed three grouse with three shots on his next opportunity. When my luck with English setters went bad, Dave Mackey put me together with Beans, the German shorthair asleep at my feet right now.

About midway in the group's eighteen years together, McIntosh split off for reasons that are important but not here. Nevertheless, we continued to hunt together. Through him I met Dale Spartas, an outdoor photographer. Dale is also a human pointer. The pointer is to the English setter what a Ferrari is to a Rolls Royce. Dale owned the first pointer that I ever saw work grouse. Her name was Ruby, and she was—and still is—a gem. That doesn't really tell what kind of a gem, which is appropriate. We hunted Ruby in the Oakey and Cow Trail covers, those islands of grouse habitat separated by grass pasture. It is a fact that, while my two shorthairs were handling their end of the deal methodically and thoroughly, Ruby tore the top off those covers, found every bird in them, and delivered a limit to Dale. On the other hand, when we went into the State Trail cover with its long expanses of wilderness, Ruby got confused. Dale called her and called her. We had no Ruby, and in this country that can be a serious problem. We have dog killers in these parts: some are timber wolves, some are coyotes, and some are outlaws. Finally, Dale was exasperated enough to reach for his shock collar.

It ought not to be funny, but slapstick comedy is a form of humor that rolls me up. Just as Dale hit the button, Ruby skidded to a halt behind him. I was looking directly at her when her eyes lit up and she came right off the ground. No amount of apologizing could heal the rift. She would have nothing to do with either of us. We skulked through the State Trail cover in the company of my methodical, logical shorthairs and killed a bunch of birds. Ruby stayed close and mumbled ugly things.

Hunting with Dale is like that. In certain covers he is spectacular; in other places he is far too much dog. He can't help it. He's a Montana guy. They have long horizons out there.

Our bird hunting time is precious. I have already written that the greatest trophy I can get from any day in the woods is six hours without a care in the world. Novelist Jim Harrison captured this island toward which all bird hunters swim when he wrote:

> If you hunt or fish a couple weeks in a row without reading newspapers or watching T.V., a certain not altogether deserved grace can reenter your life. Newsworthy events and people, as always, have gotten along in the usual ways without your mental help.

That's where the barter comes in. Hooking up with a local bird shooter who can bring to the table a string of pearls and the enthusiasm to hunt them is a commodity of value. It saves an enormous amount of time spent in large and unproductive covers or on stamped-flat public ground. The trade comes in returning to this local hunter an item of equal value. I treat my landowners with gifts, but a barter is different. The landowner provides the canvas. The local hunter provides the painting. One good Picasso deserves another.

These days I hunt alone most of the time. Those six carefree hours are not so hard to obtain if I don't have the distraction of another person's needs or expectations. Also, I can blame fate for every one of my misses and claim personal responsibility for every hit. Mostly, however, the breakup of the Missouri quail group came down to equal value in trade, which is a personal foible of mine. I am grateful for the pieces of life that I shared with my companions. They gave me a lot to write about, but those birdless quail days on public land wore away at my free-trade ideas. It wasn't always that way, as the next few chapters will illustrate.

Bob White

Bob White

Chapter Nine

For the Dog Work

Not everybody can have ruffed grouse to hunt. If they had them, they would also have the woods and terrain that support the birds. This would mean that Americans would not eat wheat, corn, beans, and other good things because there would be no field agriculture. You can cover a banquet table with all the pine needles and cones, highbush cranberry, and other woodland fibers you want, but with the possible exception of the blueberry, one loaf of fresh bread will beat them all.

Farmers need birds to hunt. That's why God created the bobwhite quail and the ring-necked pheasant and instructed them to prosper and multiply in areas that were not so woodsy. There may be other reasons, even scientific ones, but being a results-oriented guy I have settled on this explanation. But quail and pheasants do serve another purpose for bird hunters so inclined: they give southern hunters something to trade to their northern colleagues for the privilege of hunting the ruffed grouse. It's not a fair trade, you understand—bird for bird, the grouse has the quail by size almost four to one and the pheasant by taste a hundred to one. It's where they live that tips the scale to equal.

When the cover is knee-high and the only vertical parts of it are fence posts or corn stalks, a guy can actually see what he is shooting at. There is a reason for the lack of television hunting shows based around the ruffed grouse—the star is gone. Elvis has left the building, and nobody saw him go. Good grouse hunters shoot at an idea of a grouse, not the real thing. When the bird and the shotstring meet in the dog-hair aspen, success is claimed as skill. However, in those quiet moments after slipping a grouse into the game bag, honest hunters tell themselves that the shot was pure luck. When a grouse flushes, there is not much for a video camera to see.

On the other hand, the flush of a pheasant and the burst of a quail covey is getting to be a scripted item. These birds rise up shining in the sun and usually in the open. Around them is a landscape of rolling hills, golden fields, and pastoral America. Oh sure, we can focus on the troublesome cattail swamp and the interfering hedgerow, but 90 percent of the time, the space between cover and sky is blue. And thank God for it. Even a grouse-crazed bird shooter needs a break once in a while.

I shot my first quail during the mid-1970s in Iowa in the company of a fine bird hunter named Jerome Biebeshiemer. We became acquainted through the fledgling pages of the Ruffed Grouse Society's publication, *The Drummer*. At that time, it was a small newspaper printed on pulp and circulated among a membership that was hardly a good turnout at one of today's banquets. I had purchased a Model 31 Remington lightweight pump-gun and was so pleased with its easy balance that I wrote a letter to the editor of the *The Drummer* for information on bird guns like it. Jerome answered, we met, and the rest became an association that has spanned almost thirty years. He sent me a gun to try; an Ithaca Model 280 English-style double barrel in 20 gauge. I used it but not well. One memorable afternoon, I missed, consecutively, five grouse in one spot and seven in another.

Jerome was a lightweight-gun fanatic. He settled on a Franchi over-and-under, and during our years together it wore four different stocks and forends. He was always looking for ways to shave ounces off the wood and would do so until one end or the other cracked. This is a curious contrast in size, because Jerome is six feet four inches tall. His constant hunting companion—therefore, mine as well on their trips to the north country—was John Baker. John exceeded six feet four by a couple more inches. Both of these big men carried small shotguns, and when they stood side by side, the guns in their hands looked like conductor's batons.

Leaving my beloved woods and Labrador retriever behind, I traveled to Mason City, Iowa, for my first quail hunt. I brought two guns with me—my usual Model 31 lightweight 12 gauge, and a Spanish 20-gauge side-by-side. Jerome and I spent the first day hunting Mason City pheasants behind his small and tireless Brittany, but the real trip was to develop the next day. Jerome, John, and I were headed for southern Iowa, to Chariton and the county of the same name, for my first quail hunt.

There is a wonderful bridge south of Knoxville, Iowa. It crosses the backwaters of the Des Moines River and offers a landscape of river cutbanks and wooded ravines. This was the kind of country that we would hunt. Jerome had landowner friends, and they had the scruffy, hilly spaces that quail liked. In this country, a mile spreads out in front of you as fence rows and corners, brush piles and weeds. Given that we were hunting with an English setter and Jerome's Brittany and that I was carrying a side-by-side 20 gauge, my first quail hunt had everything short of tweeds and a tie.

What I did not expect were quail bursting from under my feet. When the dogs pointed them, they were not "over there," they were "right here." I knew enough to pick one bird out of a covey, but my shooting was at grouse speed. My gun was empty about the time I should have begun shooting.

"Slow down," said Jerome. "Count one, two, then shoot when you are in amongst them." He dropped his two birds in my game bag.

"Walking in on a point is not all its cracked up to be," I replied.

A Bird in the Hand

My first quail fell, finally, when a group came out of a shallow draw on a reflush. They were edgy from the first rise, and the dog got too close. I cheeked the gun, followed through, and down came the bird. Jerome's Brittany picked it up, brought it to him, and he came over to me.

"A nice little male; a bird of the year. You won't need help carrying it," he said.

It covered the palm of my hand, belly up. I hefted it, folded its wings around the body, and closed my hand. "What do I do next? Add water?"

John came over, opened his little 20 gauge, and patted me on the back. "Legend has it that the quail is so rich in taste that a man can only eat two or three."

"How many can you eat at a sitting?" I asked him.

"Oh, about ten. Har, har, har." John's laugh could be heard in Ottumwa. "I'm in it for the dog work."

I never returned to southern Iowa. Time and circumstances gave me a fine, little English setter that I named Salty and a fondness for side-by-side shotguns. In addition, during the 1980s and '90s, Missouri had bobwhite quail in bragging numbers.

It might be possible to hunt quail without dogs, but I've never seen it done. You can do it with grouse by walking slowly and stopping often. You can do it with pheasants by using a blocking edge or enough hunters to drive a field with a few standing at the end to force a flush. But quail have a tendency to stick tight. Sometimes they hold so tight that even an experienced dog can't find them.

By way of example, during one Missouri quail hunt Salty and I crossed a creek bottom and emerged on the other side. The wind was at our back, and the side of the draw that was ours to walk toward the road was grown up in fescue grass. Fescue is to the earth what carpet is to hardwood floors, a stiff and sterile covering. I had seen a covey fly through the creek-bottom trees and into the pasture, and I knew that I was far enough over to put their short-grass landing spot between me and the road's culvert. Working quail with the wind at your back is not a good tactic, but those were the cards that we had been dealt. They did not play well. We got to the road without a point or even a stumble flush.

"About face, white dog," I said," we'll try them into the wind."

We returned across the same ground, and she pointed within twenty feet. Three quail came out of the green carpeting, and two fell. Salty was not a good retriever, so I collected them. Five feet from where I picked up the last bird, she pointed again. It was a single, and it dropped like the first two. Twenty yards farther she pointed a third time, and five came up. This went on until I had collected six birds to fill the remainder of my eight-bird limit. I called Salty in, then we recrossed the creek bottom and quit. That covey had let us pass right through the middle of them.

My Missouri friends believed that if the bird work was worth doing, ten dogs must be better than one. Spence Turner would run two or three English setters at a time. Joel Vance often had two Brittanies, sometimes three, and once five. On later trips, I had my setter, Salty; Mike McIntosh ran a Brittany; and Dave Mackey hunted with his German shorthair. I guess you could say that, like Jerome's friend John Baker, they were in it for the dog work, too.

With that many candidates and plenty of open space to fool around in, the dog-work spectrum was full. I clearly remember my first Missouri quail. Thanks to my Iowa hunt, I had a rough idea of the quail game. Spence had permission to hunt on a farm north of Columbia. In a corner of this farm was a gravel pit, an area of steep cuts and draws above the flat agricultural field. He had two setters in front of us. Joel and Mike were probably around with their dogs, but Spence's setters were carrying the weight. His young female Samantha made a stylish point on a rocky sidehill. I walked in on my first Missouri quail; it came up, and I killed it. Samantha ran to pick it up. Very lovely. Then she paused, saw that I was not Spence, looked left and right, then ate the bird. I can still see the splayed toes of the quail's tiny feet as they bounced up and down in the dog's mouth. Spence came over.

"Did you get it?" he asked.

"Yep."

He looked at Samantha standing there swinging her tail. "Well, do you have it?"

"Nope."

"Where is it?"

"Dog has it."

"I don't see it," he replied.

"Nope, can't be seen."

"Why not?"

"It's in the dog," I answered casually.

Sometimes we had help from volunteer dogs. We used to hunt at Glenn's farm, an overgrown holding of lowland crop fields. The house had had paint on it at one time, but it was long gone. Glenn and his wife lived in the house. She had been crippled by a falling tree, so Glenn rented the farmland and took care of her. A pointer lived at the farm in a fifty-gallon oil drum tipped on its side in a pen. Pigs also lived in the pen, but I believe the barrel was the pointer's alone. His name was Old Smoke. He was a bug-eyed and barrel-chested dog, with a tail that had been broken at least twice and had healed crooked both times.

"Usta be a pretty good hunter, then he got old lak me," said Glenn. "He'll prolly come along with ya. Jes send 'im home."

Well, he was coming along, of that I was certain. He walked right through the pack and headed down the hill. I had no dog on this first trip, so I decided to follow him—I always bet on the local guy to find the birds. Smoke didn't stand on ceremony, he went right to them. The setters and Brittanies were making grand sweeps, but Old Smoke had the birds. There could be no doubt of that. Every kink in his broken tail was straightened out high and vertical, and all of his creaky joints were locked tight and quivering. Old Smoke was on point, and five other dogs were honoring him. The quail came out of the hedgerow, and, since we had ample time to arrange ourselves, a few must have died. Smoke did not do any retrieving. With a passing glance that said "my work here is done," he returned to his barrel.

We did not find any more quail at Glenn's place that day. The next year, I returned with Salty, my pup out of Spence Turner's Samantha. Old Smoke was gone, and Glenn did not meet us as he had the year before, so I did not find out what happened to either of them. We hunted the fields and the river bottom, and raised one covey out of harvested millet. I slid down into the creek bottom and let young Salty run the top of the bank. After one sweep, she did not come back to the edge. I lifted myself up on my toes and peeked over the top. There was an old, open-fronted lean-to facing to my right—a hog house, paintless and bent. In front of it a skinny, white setter was on point and looking into the doorway. I laid my gun on the top of the bank and crawled up the side.

"This better not be a skunk," I warned.

Salty rolled her eyes and took one step forward. I came in from the side expecting a possum or a cat, anything but what was there. When I rounded the corner, I saw the floor of the hog house literally move. It was full of quail. They wanted out, and I was in the way. Quail roared past my head, one struck my hat, and I fell over backward. I didn't see it, but I'll bet Salty rolled her eyes again.

Missouri bottomland met Salty and I the next year as well. This time we were in the Black River Creek bottoms hunting a high-hilled crop field that overlooked the river. The farmer was a young version of old Glenn. He, also, had a bird dog living amongst his hogs. This was Holly. She was white with speckles and ran on three legs, carrying her right-front leg high because it had healed crooked after she was hit by a car. She had a "sickle" tail—a sign of defective genetics to the highborn of the breed—that curled back toward her head when she pointed.

Salty and I had worked two coveys out of the field, while Spence and his companion drove the edge looking for one of the guy's big-going setters. We slid down the side of the hill into a bottom of assorted shrubs and tall, yellow grass. I set my gun down, found a soft spot, and filled my pipe. Salty flopped down for a well-deserved rest. We had moved a lot of quail but had only two in the vest. I had the tobacco going when I heard a "chuffing" sound coming down the hill toward us. In a couple minutes we were joined by Holly.

"Welcome, welcome. You are one cute little dog," I said and patted her head. She wagged her tail happily, went off about fifteen feet, and pointed.

"Must be a mouse," I said to Salty. "Still and all, no guts, no air medal." I closed my gun and stepped up beside the small, speckled dog. A single came up, and I shot it. Holly ran out and got the bird, brought it back and dropped it on the ground, then trotted to another spot. She pointed again. Salty stood up, but stayed.

This time I was a believer. Another single came out of the grass and died for its mistake. Holly retrieved the bird.

"Well, I think we are in the presence of the world's greatest singles dog," I said. "Hunt 'em up, and I'll follow."

I killed six quail with six shots over six points, one after another—bird up, bird down, bird back. Salty did not move. Holly took all the ground and got it done.

I guess we cleaned them out, because I couldn't have stopped her. When I pocketed the last of the six, she came over for a head rubbing, then three-legged her way back up the hill to her farm.

When I get to the pearly gates, if Saint Peter asks me what I want, I'll have a question for him: "Do you have any pointing dogs up here?"

If he wants to know why, I'll say, "I want to go where they went."

Chapter Ten

The Public Teat

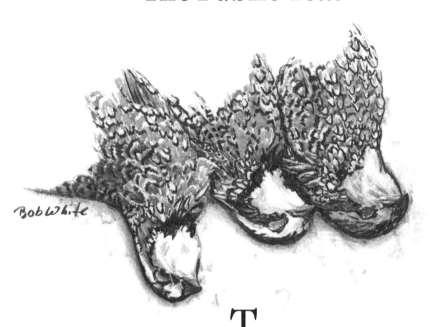

Bob White

There is a building—gray, as I remember it—in Columbia, Missouri. The building's entry opens into a lobby. Nothing comfortable, you understand; this is not a hotel. On one of the lobby's walls is the head of the largest atypical buck taken up to that date. It's a monster. It died when it got those enormous, messy antlers caught in a wire fence. The deer grew up right next to St. Louis, avoided man long enough to grow a set of antlers that big, and died in an accident. Because the whitetail met its end out of season, or in season but out of the right zone, the state of Missouri got the rack. The big-game wildlife biologist was surprised to see a deer that large, and he is the guy that they pay to know those things.

This is the building where Spence Turner worked as the state trout biologist. He shared an office with another fish guy, but most of his time was spent in the lab or out on the streams. Just a few doors away was the state quail biologist. At the time, I took this to be a good omen—a nearby colleague with all the information and population densities for bobwhite quail in the state of Missouri.

There is a second building located in Jefferson City, Missouri. This one is much nicer than Spence's workplace. It is the home of the Missouri Department of Conservation's information division. It had a dark, multicolored brick exterior and a plaza that harbored Canada geese and a few dozen ducks. Joel Vance and Mike McIntosh worked in glass-windowed offices within a few feet of the cattails and waterfowl. I took this to be a good omen, also. This building was the clearinghouse for all of the quail data gathered by the bobwhite biologist in Columbia. In these three guys, I had raw material, manufacture, and distribution.

I suppose it's possible to own too much. What's that old saying? A man with one watch knows what time it is; a man with two watches is never quite sure. If official state information was the milk of finding quail on public land, these three should have had the teat between their teeth.

Joel, Spence, and Mike lived near their work. Therefore, at least two or three days in each of my first five years of quail hunting took place in central Missouri on public management areas. There were private-land exceptions to this rule, but only a few. I missed a year after those first five, and thereafter I hunted in their company as guests of Dave Mackey in northeastern Missouri. I recall hunting only one public area in the northeastern part of the state. Dave Mackey was a quail hunter; he scouted the birds and hunted them on the private land where they lived. The public area was where my other three friends would take me when Dave was working.

In my experience, Missouri's public areas had a hard bosom. For instance, the best thing about the Prairie Home Wildlife Management Area was the gooseberry pie in Mary's Cafe. Joel, my Iowa friend Jerome, and I walked the rounded hills and valleys of Prairie Home for an entire afternoon. I recall that we found two good old boys with bony pointers and five-shot automatics. We also found my first Osage orange, and I made the mistake of cutting it open to see what was inside. The white sap is a good substitute for tar. When quail hunting reaches the stage of slicing Osage oranges, it is not good. Walking away from a point with the certainty that the dog has a mouse, and being right every time, is double not-good. But the gooseberry pie? Now, that was good. There are a lot of those old storefronts in Missouri, usually on streets where a dog could sleep and not have to move. In Mary's Cafe, the walls are decorated with completed jigsaw puzzles—the one-thousand-piece kind. Mary and her friend had put them together in the cafe, glued them to cardboard, and nailed them up. Customers and quail are rare in Prairie Home.

I remember Davisdale Wildlife Management Area because it was behind an old country church and was laid out with an agricultural appearance. It had alternating rows of corn, sorghum, and lespedeza divided by the harvested strips that the state gave the farmer for putting in the crop.

I remember one day there that was uncommonly warm and sunny. The weather in Minnesota had been ten degrees below zero when I had left the day before. Mike McIntosh and I were lying on a pond bank like lazy mud turtles. I needed the sun, and he just liked to lie down in different places. Hunting quail with Mike is like reading the Encyclopedia Britannica. You may be looking for one particular thing, but there are always distractions and detours in the way—like lying in the sun and learning the second verse of the Kingston Trio song "The John Birch Society," and finding ancient arrowheads.

I swear, the Native Americans in that part of Missouri must have lined up shoulder to shoulder and marched across the land making arrowheads, then dropping them to the ground. Perhaps they were the first bad shots in the world. If so, the game population must have been prodigious. Either way, Mike has the "eye" and can spot a point or chipped-stone edge in the most uncanny way.

We had flushed a covey of wild-and-edgy quail into a wooded creek bottom. The other fellows were over the hill, so Mike and I walked down into the heavy cover to see about a reflush. I was leading, stepping back and forth across the little watercourse. There were eroded cuts in the bank, like cracks in a sidewalk, branching off the main channel. Over the top of us, the tree branches interlaced and made an aisle. Untidy and cluttered, for a fact, but a passageway that let the sun shine through in shafts and patches. The mud bank was slightly higher than my cap. I had stopped to peer up a side cut when Mike, standing just behind my right shoulder, reached over and within two feet of my head plucked a long, perfect, white stone spearhead out of the dirt.

" I saw a small, light-colored tip," he said, rubbing the dirt from each side of the spearhead. "And look at this!"

"It looks brand new," I said. "I've never seen one found before, and you pulled it out of the dirt right before my eyes."

"It's very rare that I find one this pristine. Usually it's a tip or a broken blade," he replied, then gave me the name of the stone and the scientific classification.

Mike had reached a balance with the wildlife management areas. He had broadened the purpose of his hunts. Killing a quail was okay, and I did that by taking a bird that flushed out of the same draw, but finding a spearhead was okay too. I threatened to put a large sign on his back—*This Hunter Stops for Artifacts*—so that I wouldn't get excited whenever he hesitated.

Wildlife management areas have some positive things. They are big, so it takes a day to hunt one thoroughly. Sometimes they actually hold quail. Often they are close to a cafe that has good pie. Those three qualities define the Lamine Wildlife Management Area.

The Lamine was Joel Vance's Missouri version of the Wagon Wheel cover. He could play it like an old guitar. I can't tell you which side of the Lamine was better, or even where a side started. I just followed Joel; he followed his Brittanies; they followed their noses; and, one day, they pulled us all into a cocklebur field. The crops had surrendered early, giving up the state-subsidized fertilizer to the dominant predator—cockleburs. The stalks topped six feet, and the quail were among them. Therefore, the dogs were in them as well. The pointing-dog owner makes his compact early: "where you go, I will follow." I had burrs in places that I didn't know you get them. I had them on top of my hat, and I had a handful under each arm. I always tuck my pants into my boot socks, so each boot had a bristly cuff around its top.

Spence had run two setters into one end of the field. When we came out of the other end, neither dog could even wag its tail. The burrs had weighed them down to the ground. I have quit hunting because of rain, cold, and snow, but until that day I had never quit because of cockleburs. The dogs could not go on—their paws were full, and their inner legs were rubbed raw. We pulled out burrs until the dogs would tolerate no more abuse. I have since studied the problem. A steel-toothed comb or a matsplitter and a shot of aerosol frying-pan oil will get them out of hair, yours and the dog's, with ease. On the other hand, I pointed out to the guy that gave me the tip, a dog smelling like frying-pan oil might send an alarming message to the quail.

The Lamine could be as good as quail hunting gets. I once followed Joel and his Brittanies to a full limit in three hours. We put up ten coveys, all pointed, and I shot three consecutive doubles. John's Cafe in Otterville offered pie that was as good as it can get. No matter what, we broke at noon for pie. John's also had, in descending order of importance from pie, good-looking waitresses and good storytellers around the tables.

I preferred the Dutch apple pie, and my waitress for those few years had legs that belonged in the Louvre. During one of our noon breaks, a conservation officer sat at our table. The black-powder deer season was open, and the officer's brother-in-law had decided to try his hand.

"He had never fired a black-powder rifle, and he's not the kind of guy to ask anyone for help. So, he worked up a load that didn't kick much and seemed to throw the lead ball where the sights pointed." The officer shifted his coffee cup to the other side of his plate. "Pass the sugar, please.

"He's up in his tree stand, yesterday, and along comes a little buck walking right on the trail. He lets it get closer and closer, then decides to shoot it through the head. He fires, smoke puffs out, and the deer staggers. He can see a small black spot right between the horns." The officer shakes his head from side to side and stirs his coffee.

"The deer is still on its feet. So my brother-in-law says, 'Oh my,' grabs a lead ball, sticks it in the barrel, rams it down, then remembers that he forgot to put in the powder." We all started to laugh.

"I mean, put yourself in the hooves of this deer. You're walking along, enjoying the day, then Wham! Instant headache."

"The deer staggers off, and all the guy can do is watch it go. So he comes to me and wants to know what went wrong?"

By now we are all laughing, and it takes awhile to hear the answer.

" 'Show me the rifle,' " I tell him.

" 'Did you take the ball out?' " I ask.

" 'Yep,' he answers."

"Okay. How much powder did you use?"

" 'Oh,' he says, 'about this much.' " The officer pours a measure of sugar into his palm. It was the size of a bottle cap.

" 'Put it in there with a patch and ball, then shoot that shed door,' " I told him. " 'Boom!' goes the gun, but the ball doesn't even go through the half-inch pine. He'd been shooting those squib loads all summer and having a grand time."

There has never been a shortage of deer in Missouri, so the state takes a broad view of deer kills, being a benevolent breast of public kindness. A conservation officer can issue a possession permit for a deer that has been killed by a car or for some common-sense reason. We got five of them in two days of quail hunting. Yes, I know—the conservation officer asked the same question when we came to get the last permit.

The first one was a young doe chased out of a draw by Joel's Brittanies. It tried to jump a four-bottom plow but didn't make it, fell into the steel gridwork, and broke its back. Dave Mackey killed it quickly with a close-range shot to the head . He dressed it, and we loaded it into Spence's pickup. The conservation officer's house was on the way to our next cover, so we stopped for a permit and were on our way.

Joel's Brittanies cornered a wounded buck (the rifle season had just closed) in a creek bottom. It took some maneuvering, but Dave got another close shot to the head. We booked our second deer.

"Are you boys gettin' any quail?" the officer asked.

"Oh, yessir, a few."

We hunted a series of creek bottoms and tree lines the second day. Dave's German shorthair turned down a feeder draw, and within a few seconds a six-point buck trotted out with the short-hair right behind it. I could have touched the deer when it went by me. Reaching the fence corner, it tried to jump but fell over the top wire and broke one of its antlers. Dave walked up to the buck as it regained its feet. He slapped its hindquarters, and it spun around and hooked at him. At that point Dave's shorthair decided to revisit its early genetics and dove in, seizing the deer by the neck and dragging it down. Dave got the dog to back off and, for the third time in two days, shot a deer.

"Well," he said, "ah'm gonna to leave this one for Larry's dog food. (Larry was the landowner.) Ah'll tell him about it when we git to the house. This 'un was sick."

At sundown we had reached the tall hill on the far side of Larry's property. We crested it and started down the other side. I looked ahead and saw my little setter stopped but not on point. A closer look revealed why.

"There's another deer up here in the fence," I called. I was wrong—there was one in the fence and a second lying close by. The first deer's antlers were caught in the wires, but not because he stuck them there. He had been shot, made it over the top of the hill, and fell into the strands with his head high. He had good reason to hold up his head. He was a twelve pointer with a perfect, balanced, heavy rack that anyone would be proud to have on the wall. Ten yards away was an eight-point buck with a rack not quite as wide but just as high.

Dave looked down at the two of them. "Some SOB in that stand over there," he pointed to a box on stilts about two hundred yards away, "shot at these and never walked over here to check them out. What a waste."

We returned to the warden's house. He looked at our sheepish grins.

"Warden, the last three deer aren't fit to keep," I said. "We're just telling you that the antlers ought to be cut off and kept for school kids to see or for someone to use."

"I'll drive out tomorrow and get the horns. Here's a permit for the third one. Just one question, boys. Are you sure you're hunting quail?"

Dave answered, because some things are better left to a local. "We're huntin' quail, but we're havin' better luck with deer."

Chapter Eleven

Mack the Knife

Boblhite

If you are reading this, you know about small towns and local cafes. Add a '57 Chevy and cool, crowded Friday nights after the football game, and you know what Dave Mackey meant when he said:"I put up the collar of my letterman's jacket, walked in the door of the cafe, went up to the juke box, dropped a quarter in the slot, and played 'Mack the Knife.'"

If you don't know the song, punch it up on your computer, close your eyes, and listen to words that say,"The line forms on the right, girls...now that Macky's back in town."

I'll have a cheeseburger and a coke,Wendy, and hold the onions.

When I first met him, Dave was the headman at the Agriculture, Soil and Conservation Service office that was housed in a gray green tin building next to the Farm Store in Edina, Missouri. Edina is east of Kirksville, clinging to what's left of Missouri's small family farms and the rolling hills in the northeastern quarter of the state. The flatland belongs to the landowning corporations; the hills and draws belong to Dave's people. They do what they can to get by, just like the quail that live on the pieces of ground that the big plows can't reach.

Between the empty storefronts of feed-and-seed companies and the dust blowing down the street, are the small towns of Missouri. The town of Baring was like that. There were three empty brick buildings backed up to rusty railroad tracks, plus a bank, a grain exchange, and a hardware store. Across the street was Jake's Bar, fronting peeled white paint and a picture window advertising "Beer" and "Eats."

Inside the front door, which squeaked on opening and slammed shut, three women at a table watched a soap opera. One of them rose slowly, brought menus, and asked what we wanted to drink.

"Half-and-half (ice tea and lemonade), two coffees, and a coke. The special is on the wall. I'll be back for your order," she said.

The cook had a hairnet and wore nylon stockings rolled down below her knees. "Betty," she said to our waitress, "I told you she was going to leave him for that doctor, and he doesn't know that she's pregnant with his brother's child!"

Betty must have had something to say about that, but I was busy reading the chalkboard special that said "Burger Lattuce Fries and 3 Sides."

"I'll have the special," I told the waitress. Mike McIntosh ordered something else, then said, "I just want one side dish—peaches."

"Well, honey," she said, "you're gonna git all three whether you order 'em or not."

And that's the way it is in small-town Missouri. You get more than you want. And sometimes you get things you never expected.

"Waitress, where's the lettuce for this burger?" I asked.

"Rat there," she replied.

I looked at the plate a second time: one burger, three side dishes—peaches, cottage cheese, and glorified rice—and some round fries with square holes in them.

"I'm sorry, but I don't see the lettuce," I answered.

"There, next to the burger." She was stunned by my ignorance.

"What's next to the burger?" I asked.

"The lattice fries! You know, lattuce fries, like the sign sez." That got quite a chuckle over at the soap-opera table. Dave enjoyed it too.

Keeping Dave happy was important when we were hunting in that part of Missouri—he was the key to all the farm gates. The only public land was the Siever Wildlife Management Area. When I think of the Siever now, my hands twitch. My fingers remember the cold coming with the evening wind and about a half-dozen quail left to clean. There's something in bird blood that draws the warmth out of hands. Feathers and entrails are best kept out of pockets, so there is no relief until the job is done. A white-tailed deer laid out on snow is more work, but it is also a place to thaw out numb fingers. There was one other chilling element: I found the dried skeleton of a bird dog, still wearing its collar, with a ragged hole in its head. I never liked hunting the Siever after that.

But I liked hunting with Dave Mackey. Wearing rubber knee boots, canvas bib overalls, and an orange, hooded sweatshirt, Dave was without pretense. He used German shorthairs because they worked, and he shot a Winchester pump gun—a Model 1200 in 20 gauge—for the same reason. On a covey rise, you could expect three birds to fall to his shotgun. He didn't like beepers, shouting, whistles, or lost tempers, but that doesn't mean he didn't find all that funny. With Joel and Spence around, he laughed a lot. I laughed with him, at least when the quail were plentiful.

Dave has the sound of the south in his voice. I am from Minnesota, so I speak perfect English. One day on our way in for lunch (quail hunters never brown-bag it; they like to stop at little cafes) we were having a discussion about how things are pronounced. We pulled up in front of Jones' Grocery in a small cluster of buildings across from a city park that was complete with a bandstand suitable for a movie set.

"Okay," I said and pointed to the town sign. "What's the name of this town?"

He had been laughing about a conversation I had with Walt Olson when Dave had been to Minnesota for a grouse hunt. I recall the day. Walt had driven up on his three-wheeler, and we had gossiped about local people and the weather. Afterward, Dave, who had been pretending to sleep in the sun, rolled over and said, "Ah jist lak to lissen to him. He has sech a nice aksent."

"Wal'" he said, "you first, what's it say?"

"It's Newerk," I said, "like the place in New Jersey."

"Wrong!" Dave answered. "It's New-Ark."

We walked through the grocery part of the building to the lunch counter in a back room. Greetings were exchanged. Dave placed an order, but the woman changed it and scolded him for selecting things that "warn't good for him."

"Tell this narwegian how to pronounce the name of this town," he asked.

"It's New-Ark," she said.

"There you have it," Dave answered. "You got to learn to speak rat."

Regardless of the town's name, the fried chicken was as good as home, and so were the three side dishes, whether we wanted them or not.

The covers around Newark are gone, now—the hilltops have been plowed into the draws. When Dave and I hunted it, the crop fields were veined with small, brush-choked ravines leading into deeper cuts, and these, in turn, into creek bottoms. The farmer had left a food plot of crops at the head end of each ravine. The main yield of corn had been harvested, and that afternoon it stayed cold enough to keep the clay gumbo firm and dusty. You can carry a lot of Missouri around with you on your feet if the soil is wet.

"There're seven kinds of clay in this county," Dave declared. "Five of them crack wide open, one doubles its size, and the other will swallow you whole."

I was an expert on the characteristics of the clays of Missouri, having carried or scraped my weight from the bottom of my boots. If the day was wet, I wore my Bean Boots because the modest chain tread did not pick up as much mud when the ground was soft. If the day was frozen, I would put on my stiff-soled lug boots. The bottoms gave me better support for walking across frozen plow ruts. Of course, in Missouri you can have both kinds of weather in one day. I thought about wearing one kind of boot on each foot to cut the work in half. I exaggerate, but only to emphasize that there is a tendon inside and below your knee, and when the clay of Missouri is one way or the other, or both, with each step that tendon will let you know that you made the wrong choice.

Wet ground was not a factor in our hunt at Newark that day. Neither were beepers, shouting, whistles, or lost tempers. Dave and I went one way, Joel and Spence went the other. I watched them depart, happy with the opportunity to hunt my setter, Salty, with Dave's shorthair, Tubby.

"Cry havoc! and let slip the dogs of war." I shouted after Joel and Spence as three Brittanies and two setters carrying five chiming, beeping, or hawk-screaming collars spread out like a wolf pack, fortunately, in the opposite direction.

Before us lay the remaining three hours of the day and the crop-field draws, one after the other. We stood for a moment, savoring the silence. I heard the action of Dave's pump gun slide shut. "It's time," he said. I closed my quail gun, a 1914 L.C. Smith 4E side-by-side, a veteran of three consecutive quail doubles, and many singles. "Hunt 'em up, Salty."

"I shot behind him," I said to Dave, as if knowing what I did wrong made it acceptable or even positive. He was picking up the second bird of a double as Tubby dug around in the grass for the first fall. The covey had been pointed by both dogs out in the tip of the second draw. Actually it had been two coveys. The first flushed early, made uneasy by our noisy start, then settled in on top of its neighbors.

With Dave's double in the game bag, we had fourteen empty slots to fill our limit of sixteen birds, or eight apiece. "I thought I saw your bird flinch," answered Dave. "Don't matter, he'll be over the next hill if you got him."

Tubby was on point, standing on four, firm Teutonic legs. Salty probed the far side of the ditch. Short game and long, we had the quail on their heels. I walked in for the shot.

"It's a rabbit," I said, "I can see it standing there."

"Naw, Tubby doesn't point rabbits," Dave laughed. "She chases 'em!"

"Okay, let's see what she has," I answered, "besides the rabbit."

It was a dead cock quail, a long line of bright blood running down its breast. I picked it up and raised it for Dave to see. He waved in acknowledgment. It had been heart shot, set its wings, and skidded to a halt at the feet of the bunny. I don't know if rabbits think much, but the circumstances must have given that one some pause. Three birds down, eleven to go, and Salty had the next bunch located. She was turned almost double in a point that screamed "right here."

It was a smaller group than the first—maybe a dozen birds—and was made even smaller by three shots. I took one that rose late and broke to the open, dropping it in the frozen field where it flipped and flopped until Salty came over and put her foot on it. The others had stayed inside the tree line and went on all sides of Dave.

He held up one quail, then smiled and shrugged his shoulders. A lucky bird was still flying with its mates as they bent back to the draws we had already covered. Dave pointed forward to the next line of locust trees. We had nine more quail to claim and all the time in the world to claim them.

When we finished each finger of a main draw, we would join up at the tip, one hunter and his dog coming from each side.

"Pretty quiet in the east," said Dave.

"You mean like there's not much shooting?"

"Thas what I mean," he said, and we both laughed.

Salty wore a bell, a fine bronze one, with a pleasant tone. Except for the scratching of dog feet on hard ground and the rattle of an occasional rock, nothing else could betray our coming. We split up at the base of each ravine and worked the sides to the tip. Dave and I both doubled on the next point. Sometimes a covey will rise up and become dark marks against blue sky. When folks talk about good old boys knocking down five quail with five-shot automatics, that is the situation that gives them the chance. Five left to finish.

"Bird's up!" came the yell from across the trees. In a heart beat I had quail all around me, as if Dave had fired a cannon full of them. The black-and-white head of a cock bird must have sparkled in a certain light—it was his last fashion statement. "Got one, how about you?" I called back.

"Nothin' yet," he said, then dropped a late riser rooted out by Tubby from the tangle in the ditch bottom.

We met at the food plot in a flat spot just beyond the grassy end of the draw.

"Three more and we're tapped out," I said. "Who's gonna get the odd one?" Dave answered, then laughed and pointed to a white tail sticking straight up above the crest of the hill. That's all we could see. We didn't say it out loud, but we both mouthed the word "Point!"

It was a bowl, like a little stadium, with a patch of foxtail and weeds in the bottom. Dave and I walked down the sides. Salty, standing on top, had been honoring Tubby's point.

When the covey of quail came up, it was sound as much as sight. An intense noise, not a whirring of wings, but more like a ripping of sturdy cloth. Two fell at the first shot, and one fell at the second. We had doubled on the second bird. It's funny how that works. You would think two hunters would select two different birds. People that study this sort of phenomena believe the same thing happens when predators pick out one animal from a herd. A good theory, I guess, but I doubt that anyone interviews the lions.

We collected our birds, opened our guns, and looked at our watches. "Two hours, seven points, and fourteen quail," I told Dave. "I'd say we can consider this day seized."

"Um hmmm," he said. " Now, that's what I call a quail hunt!"

Chapter Twelve

The Gatekeeper

Have you ever wondered about abandoned houses—those structures that have outlived friends and kin? The family leaves, or one member stays and closes room after room until the world becomes the kitchen and a small bedroom.

The house at Gorin had a lot of rooms on its two floors, along with a fine, pillared porch overlooking a sidewalk lined with one-hundred-year-old cedars. The people that lived there hadn't framed a shack squatting like a muskrat on a pile of mud. This house was put on top of its hill to cast a morning shadow all the way across their flat bottom land. House and land seemed to say come up my causeway road and see me, and, as long as you're coming up, look at the crops I have grown. A craftsman had cut and shaped each spindle, putting them in a row along the front edge of the porch roof, slanted on the sides, straight over the steps. Just off the back door of the summer kitchen, the tall, metal case of a cistern crank stood in the shadow of a windmill. The pump was shaped like a tombstone, and the word "Gem" was drilled into the top of the housing.

"This was Fairview Farm," Dave said, putting his shotgun down on the porch rail.

"They named it right," I replied. "How far is it across the crop field?"

"It's a mile square. Those fields hold the spring runoff. See the dikes on each side?" A light November snow had whitened the surface. It looked like a frozen lake.

"Yes," I said, "the dikes remind me of a rice paddy."

"Sometimes the quail will get out there along those berms, but not today. It's too cold. They'll be in the draws behind the house." Dave turned back and picked up his gun. "Let's move down into the trees."

I have this lasting memory of the hill that was Fairview Farm. I remember it in the simple act of three men and two dogs—Dave, Tom Kuschel, and I led by Salty and Tubby. The three of us were spread out in a line, in the manner natural to most bird hunters, swishing through the waist-high brome while the dogs quartered in front. No one expected a covey to be on the hillside.

I was last in line, on the bottom, and looking up the moment the quail lifted off. They did not flush as a single burst. Instead, they came up in a wave, starting near Dave and rolling downhill until the birds closest to me were flying below those still coming up. Behind them rose the dignified but scuffed walls of the main house, both chimneys still proud against the gray sky, and a black barn-roof next to the vine-covered windmill. One glance took it all in, then it was time to concentrate on a quartet of quail banking from right to left. As I swung, small brown rockets were stopped in midair by the other guns. I suppose I did my share, too, but an important part of the picture in my mind was missing. Who were the people of Fairview Farm?

Across the valley, two farms were clustered on a hilltop. Those two, plus some others, were owned by a corporation. The farm manager, a friend of Dave's named Larry Paisley, allowed us on the land. Larry was a quail hunter; thus, the top of each of the property's ravines had a food plot. There were no people at home in the buildings, but there were quail at home on the land. Larry's hand was evident wherever we went. He even had pheasants, and in Scotland County, Missouri, at that time a hunter could shoot two—in theory. In practice, the hunter had to get there before the dogs.

The main barn on the second Paisley farm was square and solid on the hilltop, surrounded by a jungle of weeds that had volunteered from the old cattle yard. When driving up from the west, as we were doing, the rising sun was behind the barn casting a shadow across the driveway but leaving everything else in a dazzling, snowy lacework. Dave had had two thoughts over breakfast: the pheasants would be in the cattle-yard weeds; and we were going to stop short of the old house, get out quietly, and catch the whole flock in the open—in theory. In practice, he failed to reckon with the pent-up energy of Spence Turner's setters.

I can see it today: a dazzle of sparkling sunrise weed-tops, the great, dark hulk of the barn, and two, maybe three, setters streaking into the white fairyland. We were running silent—no shouting, no beeping, no whistling. And in three seconds, no pheasants.

"Oh Lawd," I heard Dave shout. "There they go!"

The whole flock of twenty or thirty birds was climbing out of the thistles and cockleburs, gone to the wide land below.

"You can call the dogs back, now," a voice said.

Then there was Spence yelling, "C'mon around," and tooting hard on his whistle. Two dogs came back, or maybe one. That's the thing about setters; the big-going ones cover enough of the earth that it could be the same dog on its second lap.

"Are those pheasants out there by the far fence?" I asked.

"Where?" someone asked.

"Look out to the horizon, see all those spots. Right there," I pointed to the west fence line, "above the seagull."

"That's not a gull, that's a setter."

A windowless stucco house was below the main farm, set next to a creek and close to the road. Salty and I had flushed a pheasant, clearly a scatter from the morning's mishap, that had curled around the house and flown over the high-grass ravine. We followed, not from optimism, but because I could see a food plot on the ravine's other side. Salty did not find the lone pheasant, though she did a fine job of pointing, releasing, and repointing until another bird was pinned tight. I walked close, and a quail came up, straightaway, flying right at the stucco house.

I lifted the barrels of my L.C. Smith from under the bird's tail, over the top, and slapped the front trigger. There was a puff of feathers, then the quail arced right through the middle of the empty window frame and struck the wall inside.

I lifted both arms and hollered, "Field goal!"

The earth under the back steps of the house was opened by erosion that had undercut the foundation as well. The segment under the hallway that fronted the window had collapsed into the basement. I stepped through the door and peeked around the corner. There lay my quail on the hardwood floor, belly up. It was a hen, her buff-colored head turned to the left. A small, brown feather was stuck to the plaster wall just above the bird. All that was between me and the quail was old flooring, some broken window glass, and six feet of air on top of two feet of rubble.

There was one other bit of debris on the floor—an old valentine. A corner of the paper was caught in a crack between the floor and the outside wall. It was one of those single-sheet kind, the ones we used to buy at the dime store and hand out to our grade-school classmates. The head of the hen quail appeared to be looking right at it.

Sometimes, you just have to know. A poem by Gabriel Zaid flashed into my mind:

> A coin tossed into the air
> the petals plucked from a daisy
> the open pages of a fallen book
> are not read as statistical noise
> but as signs, messages,
> a dialogue with eternity.

I took the first step, and the next one, and the next, until I picked up my quail and her page from eternity. Since I wanted to stay a while longer, I carefully retraced my exact path around the corner and out the door. I sat on the back steps, with the quail next to me, and read the valentine.

On the card was a large, red heart with the printed word "To" followed by a handwritten name, "Lucy," and held by a brown, smiling, fuzzy bear. The message was:

> You are a gift
> a friend like no other,
> for life we will be
> like sister and brother.

The valentine was signed, "Phillip," in the same back-slanted scrawl.

"Well, Salty," I said, as she sniffed the quail, "Lucy may have hoped for more, because she saved this until her people left." I found an open crack in the plaster and slipped the message into the wall. I would let fate decide who would read it again.

Fred Ewalt was not a fellow who believed in a way out. As far as he was concerned, his place was home. He made one choice, then decided to do his best with it and never think of the possibility of doing anything else. He was eighty-six years old when I met him. I had a few "firsts" on his farm.

It was the first time I actually met one of the gatekeepers. They are the people who stay; the Chosen Seed. Fred was the last of his family still on the land where they all had been grown. He was perfect because, in the words of Antoine St. Exupery, "Perfection is attained, not when there is nothing left to add, but when there is nothing left to take away." Fred had boiled life down to what was necessary. He had an old pickup, a house on the back side of worn-out, a blue-heeler dog for company, and a cat that lived on his roof. He fed the cat by putting handfuls of cat chow in the gutter outside the back door. In the yard was a tall persimmon tree. Until you have picked frost-ripened persimmons right off the branches, golden and translucent, you have not defined the word sweet. Everything Fred ate came from his garden or his farm, and when we hunted his place, he always made us lunch. An eight-course meal of beef, venison, sauerkraut, beans, potatoes and gravy, with mustard greens, tomatoes, corn bread, muffins, pumpkin pie, and pear cider. He had an L.C. Smith shotgun, a bolt-action Winchester rifle, and a Model 12 Winchester trap gun.

Fred loved to work with his lathe and his native walnut boards. He also loved a practical joke. In his trapshooting days, he and his cronies had lathed some clay pigeons out of green birch and painted them black and orange. Then they put a buddy in the trap house. It seems that one of the club members was getting a bit noisy about his shooting ability. The braggart had broken ten in a row, then they gave him the birch pigeons, one after the other. Try as he might the "clay" pigeons flew on—green birch can absorb a lot of shot. Fred said they pretty much had the braggart reduced to tears.

Fred's place was accessible over the first low-water ford I ever saw. In the spring there could be a couple of weeks where the runoff isolated him from the world. But, then, Fred's world was pretty small. His corner of it had been transformed into a quail paradise with Dave as planner and partner. Fred had a panfish lake—thanks to a dammed-up draw—and a section of native prairie uncut by plow. The farm was at that point where the last man was standing. I got the answer to my question, who lived here? A first.

We usually hunted Fred's place, as the saying goes, "suspender and belt." Joel often put all five of his Brittanies on the ground. These five together with my Salty, Dave's Tubby, and all three of Spence's setters didn't leave many square feet untrampled. That, too, was a first. Although we went in different directions, at any one time, I could have a Brittany, at least one setter, my dog, plus a covey of quail in every place one ought to be. Spence was my usual hunting partner at Fred's because he had a knowledge of how the farm was laid out. It made for several "firsts" on almost every point.

"I've never seen that happen before," could have been a motto for both good and bad. We shot a bunch of quail each year, and time was drawing to a close for Fred at the same rate. The last year we went, Fred was limited to the kitchen and a side room. As much as he wanted to, he could not make lunch. He apologized. Can you imagine? All of the challenges he faced, and he was sorry he could not take on more.

The last year I visited the Ewalt farm, Dave explained that not only were the quail absent, but Fred was gone too. It had become too much, or not enough. Either way, the house was empty. So was the farm. We didn't flush a single bird. I climbed out of the creek bottom, the same one crossed by the low-water ford, and walked the bank to join the others on a field edge. I felt a shock, electric and painful, in the muscle of my right forearm. I looked down and was startled to see a locust thorn buried about an inch in my arm. All those years walking among the prickly plants of Missouri and suddenly, at the end of a birdless day, I was stabbed. I pulled out the thorn and stuck it in my pocket. My arm still hurt like fire. "Seems about right," I said to whatever dog came running by. "Fred's gone, and it's time to get the hell out!"

Dave had seen it coming. He had bought a worn-out farm near Edina. In the last couple of years, like Fred's place in its prime, it was prospering under good management and hard work. Chigger Ridge had an old barn but no house. Dave had to have a place to catch crappies, so a draw was dammed to create a fishpond. Once the pond was in place, a little day cabin followed, and so did the quail coveys. He always had at least five on the place, sometimes more. When we had been to all the other places, Chigger Ridge was kept back for desert.

I had a first at Dave's too. The covey behind the pond was not at home that day, so Salty and I swung wide of the others to take a chance on a cluster of brush along Dave's fence across a field planted with some sort of young sprouts. That year, Dave had started a pup, Coco, a solid-brown German shorthair and a far cry from the methodical, logical Tubby. Coco believed in the principal of jet-powered flight, as in find the sound barrier and break through it.

My hunch proved to be correct; the covey was on the fence line and in the bottom of the clump of brush. I had a solid point. I turned to give a waved-hat signal to the others, when I saw a con-trail of dust coming right for me. Ahead of this jet stream was Coco. My cap remained in my hand, held at about shoulder level. I was at a loss. Dave Mackey had built the fence, and the wires were strung tight enough to pluck a tune. Bearing down on Salty and me was a canine cruise missile. If Coco hit the fence, she would go through it like a loaf of German bread through a slicer.

No problem. She launched herself at ten feet, soared through the air, over the fence, and into the covey. I would have loved to have seen that from the quail point of view. They expected the white setter, the point, the approaching hunter. It all fit so well into generations of tradition. Quail know their part. Then, this guy introduces dog artillery, a brown projectile with bright, gleaming, yellow eyes and big, white teeth. Quail flew like shell fragments.

"That's what I call a covey flush," I hollered to the others. The show had been so good that I forgot to shoot.

Within three years, I didn't have to forget. There was nothing to shoot.

Chapter Thirteen

The Lilies of the Field

Consider the lilies of the field. The Bible says they prosper and grow without the hand of man. Perhaps they survive because they hide their critical parts underground and hunker down until bad weather passes. Quail can't do that—if they can't find good cover, they die.

The Atlanta Wildlife Management Area, near Kirksville, Missouri, was clothed, sheeted, and covered in a quarter inch of clear ice. It seemed as if all the world had been solidified. As I walked through the fields, the grass would collapse in front of my boots before I stepped on it—the vibrations from my footsteps were more than the stems could bear. The dogs flushed three turkeys, startling them from their roost in the trees. I have never seen a bull in a china shop, but if a bull can break more glass than the ice those turkeys shattered flying through the coated tree branches, it must be an awesome spectacle.

There were no quail. Maybe there were none to begin with, but the area was empty. I have heard rumors of quail trotting down fox burrows to escape the weather, but the notion of a favorite meal delivering itself to the doorway of its major predator lacks common sense. It is a fact, however, that ice melts as the day warms. Rain is hot compared to the ice water that soaks hunting pants. I had a picture taken to prove that canvas turns black and lips turn blue.

I didn't have to be a mathematician to know that bad weather and apathetic management were creating fewer quail every year. A five-covey day was now considered good. To me, a covey of quail was about the same as one grouse. A bird hunter seeks both in increments of one at a time. If there are two grouse in a flush, that's a bonus. If a quail covey spreads out and can be hunted in singles and doubles, that is also a bonus. By midseason in Minnesota, I knew where every grouse was going to be in my covers. Some of them I even knew by habit and personality. But this was Missouri. Where had the quail gone? Had the ice storms killed them? Not all of them, of course; quail have been getting through ice storms for eons. I would ask my hosts.

Their answer to my question was ask Dave Mackey. Setting aside for a moment that Dave didn't owe me a thing, let alone an answer, I already knew that quail populations could recover from severe losses. Indeed, in terms of production the bobwhite quail is the workaholic of the bird world. Unfortunately, all this must happen before the November season, because the hunter stands at the distribution end of the quail factory. If the production end has been slack, or if bad information puts the hunter at the wrong factory, there is no product.

For awhile I thought it must be the turkeys—I was seeing more of them each year. At the Fairview Farm, Salty pointed a turkey so big that when it flushed from under her nose we both jumped backward three feet. Turkey points became a common event. It was a rare day when at least a dozen turkeys weren't included in the game-sighting tally.

"Dave," I said, "I think turkeys are eating the quail. Think about it. They're proving that the dinosaur was a warm-blooded relative of the bird. Turkeys in the spring are nothing more than feathered velociraptors. They're just snapping up those little quail along with grasshoppers and other bugs."

Dave set down his beer, then he picked it up and looked at the label. "Nope," he said. "There's nothin' on this can that says the more of these the user drinks, the smarter he becomes."

I could see my turkey theory wasn't working. "How about pheasants?" I asked. "We've been seeing more every year, and they like to sneak around and act dishonest."

Dave and I were having our turkeys-killing-quail discussion in his garage. It had been prompted by a one-covey day.

"We found a covey after you left," I explained. "Spence and I came in from the side closest to the road with his two setters and Beans, while the boys—Max and Tom's son, Miles—were on the far side of a brush pile. Beans pointed, and the setters honored. Then, for some reason, the setters bolted, and the covey burst up and over the brush."

"And that was it?" Dave asked.

"All gone," I answered. "No singles or scatters."

"Nothing before that or after?" he asked.

"Nothing."

That was at the end of the third day. We had been to Fred Ewalt's the day before and had drawn a blank. It was like going to the zoo and finding all the cages empty. I sat down with Spence to discuss the situation. The number of quail in Dave's private covers were precious few; we had to broaden the pressure.

"We're leaning on Dave pretty hard, Spence. I have Max, and Tom has Miles. With you, Joel, and Andy (Joel's son) that's seven hunters. Let's try some of your covers."

"I don't have any," he answered.

"Well, I know you hunt other places in this area," I said. "Let's try those."

"I'm a guest when I hunt those covers," he replied. "We could go over to the Atlanta Wildlife Management Area, but I don't know whether that's good or bad."

We hadn't reached the end of the line, but I could see it from there.

In the standard outdoor-video script, we were at that point where the actors talk about the pretty scenery and the value of spending time together. The prop manager would have to go to the game farm and get some birds to salt the fields. This, however, was reality, and as the man said, "If you can't dance, blame the band." Neither Spence nor Joel had an alternative to leaning on Dave.

The best man I knew in a spot like this was Sam Collier. Sam never saw a "No Trespassing" sign that he didn't love. Some men are born to sell. To Sam, "no" meant "know." He was sure, without a fragment of doubt, that once the farmer got to know him, permission was only a knock on the door. Sam refused to take no for an answer.

Sam Collier came into the quail-hunting years in a period between our group's giving up the covers around Columbia and the wildlife management areas around Otterville and our sole reliance on Dave Mackey. Sam was a big, dark-eyed, gregarious man who was a bottomless well of optimism. I never saw him shoot a bird, and I never saw his dog point one. But I'll bet I sat in the yard of every farm from Shelbina to Shelbyville.

Sam loved dogs. We met two hunters in the Sam-and-Spence

watering hole called Clapper's Cafe. One of their setters, the hunters said, had fallen ill. The dog's owner and his friend, both doctors, thought the dog had sipped some fouled water. They would give the dog an overnight rest and see what the next morning brought. Sounded sensible to me. The steaks were good, the bourbon better, and I was tired. About eleven that night, the festivities at Clapper's had wound down, and we boarded Sam's Chevrolet Suburban for a return to his Airstream trailer. We drove past the local motel, and Sam saw the doctors' car.

"Let's stop!" he said. "We could take the dog to a vet I know in Columbia!"

"Good idea," said Spence, "I know two vets at the University. We could be there by midnight"

"Guys," I offered my opinion, "if two doctors aren't concerned about their own dog, why are you worried?"

A conversation followed as we backed up and drove into the parking lot. The gist of it was that these things are often a lot more serious than people think. How would we feel if their dog died?

"I'd feel the way I do right now," I said. "Tired and hungover."

Sam and Spence piled out of the Suburban and pounded on the door. It opened, slightly. Explanations were made with hand gestures. I wondered how straight the road was from Shelbina to Columbia, because Sam Collier would not take a refusal. Nevertheless, that's what he got. Both of the Good Samaritans, crestfallen, came back for a quiet drive to Lentner and the Airstream.

I never saw Sam after that year. When I asked about him, Spence said he suffered some sort of business setback. I'm sure Sam's roots were in the soil, though, and he came back. The quail, however, did not.

Louis Nizer was a famous trial attorney and the author of a book entitled *The Implosion Conspiracy*. He believed that catastrophes are never the result of one big thing. Rather, they are the accumulation of small events gathering in an unexpected way, at a place and in a time that can tie them together. Dave thought that the weather was the culprit, that untimely rains had drowned the chicks. Spence thought it was poor management practices. For years, Joel had written articles warning of the decline and citing a variety of theories from fall plowing to incompetence in the United States Department of Agriculture. Regardless of the reason, Tom and I had sons who had not yet taken their first quail, and we were two days away from the end.

The menu for the night meal was supposed to be panfries and quail. I brought the venison chops in from the grill, then Tom and I talked while we washed the dinner dishes.

"I killed some quail last night. Beans and I went down to the flats along the river. There was one small covey and three or four scatters," I said.

"I wondered where you went," he replied.

"I think if we take the boys and Beans tomorrow evening, I can find them again."

"Sounds good." And it was.

The county road was a raised causeway leading off the river bridge. On both sides, the soybeans had been picked. A long ditch divided the fields and was heavy in grass, bulldozer piles, and lines of tall hardwoods for half its length. We split up—Tom, Miles, and Max on one side; the dog and I on the other.

"Walk quietly, and pick your way through the trees along the edge. Beans and I will cover the field edge. We'll take it all the way to the next road," I whispered. In spite of another empty morning and afternoon, there were nods and smiles all around.

The fall had been especially warm in Missouri, and when the temperature drops with the sunset, the air on the fields gathers in small, light clouds of fog. Some patches are still sweet from the sun blending into the cold, heavy, blue mist. A dog was barking a mile away and was not happy about his life.

When we climbed from the county-road ditch, field fog was all we had seen. Tom and Miles decided to swing wide and double back. "Max and I will walk the ditch, again," I said. They moved off, passing through a small eddy of blue air to gain the high ground on the other side. Max and I stood at rest.

"Where's Beans?" I asked. Max has better ears than I do, and Beans was wearing Salty's old bell. Max pointed across the ditch to a line of trees in the next field. Three quail whizzed by, and more spots were coming right at us!

"Take 'em, take 'em!" I hollered. Like decoying bluebill ducks, the quail bared their breasts to what was coming.

I heard two shots beside me. The last one stabbed out a pencil of fire, and beyond it a quail tumbled end over end, passing by like a feathery badminton shuttle. It fell into the log pile behind us. Max had gotten his first quail, but now the question was whether Beans could get it.

The shorthair came on a dead run, leaping the ditch and skidding to a stop by my leg. "Get any, boss?" was in his eyes.

I gestured toward the log pile and commanded, "Back!" Then I looked at Max and said, "Hope for the best."

I don't know why I was worried. Beans had the quail and was trotting back, head down and wiggling with happiness. Since he has a short tail, he would shake his whole body to make sure you knew he was pleased.

We gathered together at the road where we started. Tom and Miles had drawn another blank walk. None of the covey had settled in the field or in the ditch. They had simply vanished. The boys led the way, following Beans along the causeway.

"I saw those birds go by you," Tom said. "After they cleared the road, the bunch went right down on the deck. I could make out that little flickering of light from their wings."

A Bird in the Hand

"I thought they came this way," I said, starting my story, when Beans spun to the left, locked into a point in the ditch grass, at the same time the fugitives burst out in front of Miles. He shot his pump gun dry, as fast as it could go. His bird fell into the soybean stubble.

For the second time that evening, I was too startled to shoot. Miles looked at all of us. "Did anyone else shoot?" he asked.

"Nope," his dad answered. "You kind of filled that spot for us."

A quail apiece—a harvest of flowers in a time of thorns.

Chapter Fourteen

OK O'Toole

Sometimes things are not what they appear to be. At one time I owned a green Buick. If there was ever something that lacked a deceptive appearance, it would be a green, four-door Buick. The car was as exotic as a barnyard donkey. Like all Minnesota cars, it had a plug sticking out of the grille. When the weather got cold, you plugged the cord into an outside outlet, and a heating element in the motor kept things warm. I did this every night, and every morning the Buick started—until one morning when it didn't. In this modern age, a stalled car that has a good battery but doesn't start means a tow to the garage. Just lift the hood and look into the engine well—there might be a motor under all those hoses and covers, but there's nothing you can mess around with.

The garage called me at noon, and I walked across the street to claim my loyal, now revived, servant.

"Look under here," the mechanic said, and lifted the hood. "See this cord coming from the plug-in?"

"Sure, I see it," I replied.

He held up the motor end. It wasn't connected to anything.

Western Oklahoma is like that. This corner of Oklahoma could export red dirt and ragweed. It is the other Oklahoma, the child of bust and boom. Flatter than a day-old beer, it stretches for miles to the Texas Panhandle, working up the energy to roll a hill here and a butte over there. It looks like a crow would need a bag lunch to fly over it. But looks can be deceiving, because the land around Woodward, Oklahoma, could export one other commodity. It has enough quail to give away to the poor. It has quail enough to export.

Dennis O'Toole is like that. I started a lawsuit against an unpleasant man and his insurance company. Dennis represented the company. Dennis looks like an insurance company, or a green, four-door Buick. He is solid, dependable, unassuming, patient, and, like my old Buick, waiting with a surprise.

"Your honor," he said, "I asked for this conference in chambers because the evidence that Mr. Lundrigan seeks to introduce would prove a criminal act was done by this defendant. However, this is a civil case. It might be admissible to show the intent of this fellow, and Mr. Lundrigan would win a big judgment from this jury, but the court of appeals will throw the case out."

He was right. I did not ask for the evidence to be admitted and dismissed the part of the case affecting Mr. O'Toole's client. The insurance company, and Dennis O'Toole, went out the door. I got my judgment against the defendant, but with a less-adept defense attorney.

Dennis is from Grand Rapids, Minnesota, a nearby community,

and in the course of our thrust and parry, I learned that we shared common interests in grouse, quail, pointing dogs, and fine guns. He also has an affection for woodcock, but then, he defends insurance companies, and the two are remarkably similar.

It was February. A long time after the end of grouse season, and an even longer time to wait for the next one. I was trudging on time to my tidy fortune, as W. H. Auden would say, with no relief in sight beyond the mental company of outdoor writers on their magazine-sponsored trips. The telephone rang. It was Dennis.

"I have two things to discuss," the voice said.

"Dennis, it's nice to talk to you, too," I answered.

"I have a Fox A-grade 16 gauge and a quail-hunting trip to Oklahoma. We would leave in a week. It's a trip I ordinarily would have taken with my brothers in December, but we got canceled by an early snowstorm. The outfitter has an end-of-season opening. I'll drive, and you can visit. What do you say?"

We discussed the distance, time on the road, and the fact that I had not been quail hunting for five years. "Ten coveys a day would be average," he said, "and the outfitter prefers that you don't bring your dogs. He uses ten pointers a day. I'm going to bring my setter for company, of course."

"Of course," I replied. The thought of not having the responsibility of dogs, food, lodging, hunting covers, and success was intoxicating. "Count me in."

Bad weather is only bad in relation to what happens to you the rest of the day. Ninety cars ended up in the ditch between Minneapolis and Des Moines. We weren't one of them. It slowed us down, but I got to see the oak hills of western Iowa and the night-lights of Kansas City. We pulled over for the night in Ottawa, Kansas. It could have been any motel anywhere, with nothing to see or wait for. The next day, Wichita went by, and noon found us in Enid, Oklahoma, the home of pointing-dog field trials; the Woodring Municipal Airport; and a dented, brown, wind-scoured aircraft hangar converted to a building called Champlin Firearms. A slightly askew sign hung over the door; it said J. J. Perodeau, Gunmaker.

"I need to have the chokes opened up on the Fox," Dennis said. "There are lots of things to look at inside."

"Good thing," I replied, "because there's not much to see on the outside."

The door squeaked open into a room of tables, gun racks, barrels, stocks, tools, and blue smoke. Two men bent over their work, each nursing a cigarette. At a glance, I could see that this was not the place in the Beretta ad showing varnished wood trim and Barbour waxed clothing. We were a far piece from the cautious, low-fat, high-fiber, helmet-wearing generation. Perodeau was a Frenchman, polite but intense, focused on a Purdey shotgun lock. His faithful assistant handled the public relations and Dennis's Fox 16 gauge. Whatever money had been expended in the business had clearly gone to tools, and, as I stepped into the rooms behind the shop, I could see it had also gone into inventory.

Lions and tigers and bears—oh my—and all the guns that had taken them. Big-game and dangerous-game rifles; some modern, and some, in fact most, showing many years of wear and care. There was a Winchester Model 86 lever action in Express 50 caliber, and five or six African-game double rifles with bores as big as culverts.

Dennis walked through the door. "This is going to take awhile," he said, "they want to check the under-rib and measure the bores."

I waved him off. "Don't worry about me, take all day."

I have this theory. I believe that if I can handle all of the high-quality guns, actually pick them up and run their lines and weight through my hands, my senses will be educated and my mind will remember the feel and balance of a fine bird gun. Some day I may take an ordinary gun off the rack and discover those same qualities. Sort of like buying a Volkswagen with a Ferrari soul. The room behind the big-game rifles was lined with Fabbris, Holland and Hollands, Purdeys, and Boss shotguns. I not only got to touch the supermodels, I got to fondle them as well.

My gun of choice for the trip was a Model 12 Winchester in 16 gauge. I have a preference for solid-rib guns. When I bought this one, I was shown three Model 12 guns. A three-inch-magnum duck gun with a solid rib, a 20-gauge field gun, and the 16 gauge. I was most interested in the three-inch-magnum gun and bought it, but after handling each of the three, I liked the feel of the 16 gauge best. I bought it as well. Now, years later, the 16 gauge is all that remains of my Winchester Model 12 collection. I am of the opinion that a man with a Model 12 Winchester, who shoots it well, can put the gun in a rack with the best in the world and not be ashamed. Mine is a classic gun, slim, fast, and choked for prairie birds. It shoots where I look. My Model 12 lacks the stylish appearance of a fine double, and its receiver is silver with a few flakes of bluing left, but it handles like a rapier.

Dennis and I had left the snow behind in Kansas. It was almost mid-February, and, while there were melting piles in the shade of buildings, the ground in Oklahoma was bare. Between Enid and Woodward the country was cedar brush leading up to a line of ancient red buttes. Oil pumps bowed to one another on the opposite side of the hill country leading into Woodward. The town had seen better times. Our motel had been built when money was around—my room had enough space for a band, but the rate was strictly roadhouse level. At that price, I took a room all for myself.

"What time do we rise?" I asked.

"Be ready to go at 10 A.M.," Dennis answered, "Milt says any earlier is a waste."

I was ready at 7 A.M. All I had for a reference was eighteen years of Missouri quail hunting. (In those years, quail hunting was regulated by the rise and setting of the dogs.) At 10 A.M., promptly, Milt

Rose drove into the parking lot. He's the Chairman of the Board, Chief Financial Officer, and Minister of Transportation of North-west Hunts Guide Service.

When you look at Milt, the first thing you have to do is set aside the Martha-Stewart-goes-bird-hunting image. That's easy. He isn't wearing a broad-brimmed safari hat or matching special-event shirt and hunting trousers. His Chevy Suburban has working dirt on it, and his dog trailer is a many-years-ago model with an odd assortment of clips and dangles holding the doors shut. No pretenses with Milt. Unless the object, article, or dog furthered the purpose of the hunt, which was to kill wild quail, he didn't have it around. Milt didn't even have time for shaving. He was a bearded pair of bright, dark eyes under a baseball cap.

The essence of Oklahoma stepped out of the passenger side. This was Aaron Brock.

"Is that Erin, or Aaron?" I asked. (I needed the spelling for my journal.)

"That's Aaron," he drawled. "A-A-R-O-N, jist lak in the Bible."

Aaron would be our caretaker—the shepard of the flock, just like in the Bible. Milt planned the hunt, then Aaron executed the plan and handled the dogs.

"Now men," Milt said to Dennis and me, "I usually have four hunters, but here you are. (Two of our group had turned back, or never started). So, we'll work the small coveys, moving fast between places. We'll put up between fourteen and fifteen coveys a day. The limit is ten birds apiece. You will get your ten birds if you kill them one at a time. Don't talk to my dogs; they know their business. Put your gun cases away; we won't need them, and they get in the way. Unload your guns when we cross every fence. Shoot into blue sky and you won't hit my dogs or my guide. That's about it. The quail should be in the fencerows by now."

Pinch me, I thought. Fourteen or fifteen coveys! All I have to do is shoot straight. I am standing in my shirtsleeves in mid-February with nothing in front of me but six hours of hunting without a care in the world. A few dollars for a slice of heaven.

I opened the back door of the Suburban, slid my Model 12 into a slot next to the seat, and almost sat in a shiny pile of dog shit. "Oops!" said Milt, and reached back to pick up the plastic replica. You have to stay loose when Milt is in charge.

And you have to walk slow when Aaron is the caretaker. They wrestled two pointers out of the trailer, then a setter for the detail work. Dennis's little dog joined the group. The shock collars were strapped on, but there were no beepers that I remember. Our first hunt was on cattle range with a water tank in the foreground, blue sky above, yellow brown grass knee-high to the horizon, and an occasional stunted oak tree tied into a fence line. I loaded up and started after the pointers. I was still in my Missouri mind, which meant that I had to get to the quail about the time the pointers did, so that I could shoot birds instead of watch them fly away.

Aaron gestured to me after a half hour. I thought he was beckoning to a bird dog and looked behind. Nope, he wanted me to come over.

"You got to slow down," he said, placing a hand on my shoulder. "The dawgs will find the birds, and they'll hold 'em. Watch me."

"Okay, okay, sorry," I replied. "I'm used to something else."

I had not been in on the first covey rise next to the water tank. About twenty quail had been pointed solidly, came up, and dispersed over the hillside. Dennis had a couple shots but nothing fell. The pointers dodged and weaved through the red-dirt paths. Each one wore a pair of boots. The sand burrs in some areas of Oklahoma are like earthbound barbed wire, and even hardened dogs like these will pull up to dig at burrs between their toes. The far pointer was running across my path, and then he wasn't. I have no idea how they do that. A human athlete would topple onto his nose.

"Point!" No hollering, just Aaron saying the word and lifting his cap.

I walked over slowly, and three quail came up. I focused on one, killed it, and let the others go. The setter came off her honor point and picked up the bird, delivering it to Aaron. He put it in his vest and touched his cap brim. The best was yet to come.

While we hunted, Milt would drive over to the next place and locate the coveys. That done, he would return to our location. The dogs were watered, trailered, and the quail dropped into a five-gallon bucket. The next farm was never far.

"What are those blue fifty-gallon drums I see every now and again?" I asked.

Milt said, "Those are our feeding stations. The quail get along pretty well out here if the snow is thin, but when it piles up they suffer. We had snow last week, and I can see the quail you got have lost maybe 10 to 25 percent of their body fat. Those barrels have a feed mixture in them. Did you see where we cut fairly big holes along the bottom edge?" I acknowledged that I had seen the triangular cuts, each one maybe an inch on a side. "Commercial quail feeders scatter the seeds with a wheel. It takes a lot of quail energy to dig one frozen seed out of the ice. It isn't worth it to the bird for what it gets. Using our method, the barrel is always pouring new seed on top of the frozen stuff. They can get a lot of seed in a short time, and it saves their energy."

Milt and Aaron knew the coveys personally. We pulled up to a brushy fence corner. A short conference between them picked the dogs suited for this hunt. We crossed the fence and stepped right into the covey. A quail bomb.

"Damn, I thought they'd be farther up!" exclaimed Milt. The covey—a nice bunch of maybe fifteen to twenty birds—headed across the open, close-cropped pasture grass. The whole group hit the brakes over a grassy hilltop and pitched in.

"The other covey is out there on the water tank," said Milt.

"They joined up with them," replied Dennis, "just like Hungarian partridge do when they fly over another group."

The pointers were on their tails, charging across the yellow turf. There they go, I thought, the whole bunch will lift off and fly to Texas. The birds never had a chance—both dogs froze down, reset once, and stayed solid. It's the sort of thing I should have expected.

Walking across a winter fairway to a cover that is simply waist-high yellow grass gives a hunter a lot of time for anticipation. Somehow, I felt that I didn't deserve this. I should have been sweating and swearing.

"A covey that big does not come off all at once," Milt said, as we walked. "I'd like you boys to take as many as you can out of this bunch. It's too big to overwinter on this patch. They winter-kill and don't breed as freely as a smaller one."

"Well," I whispered to myself, "I'll do my part."

I scored a double as the first group came up. The next bunch rose in front of Dennis, giving me time to reload. The covey in the middle left their grass patch, and two more quail fell. The 16 gauge was doing its part to keep up with the dogs, and we hadn't lost or crippled a bird. The four quail were little clumps on the turf.

Aaron picked them from each dog, "Thas good shootin'."

I'm sure I made some modest response, because Aaron is not the kind of guy that one brags to. No one wants to get struck by lightning for puffing up, but inside my head, I was making high fives.

Milt probably carried ten dogs in the trailer. He selected his three players by the job at hand. We stopped at a set of abandoned buildings. The quail cover was beyond the ruins, so I walked on as Dennis and Milt paced off a known distance from the side of a shed. Dennis was having some problems with the Fox, and he wanted to check the point of impact. Two pointers, Aaron, and I topped the hill, and on the far side a lemon-and-white pointer was locked up in a small, grassy bowl of lowland. The bird went out to my left, and, simultaneously, another went flying past my head. I took the left one first, then pivoted for an easy straightaway.

Both quail were down in tall grass. The pointer found the first because he had watched it tumble. I walked slowly and carefully to a certain tall weed. "It ought to be right here," I said. "I marked it down when I took the shot." However, no amount of poking around turned up a quail. Milt doesn't allow his hunters to enter a fall area until the dogs have covered it. We were way past time on this one. Aaron walked back to the trailer and came out with a small black-and-white setter. He leashed her, then brought her to where I was standing.

"Let's try this one. If she cain't find it, it'll feed the foxes," he said. Then Milt snapped, "Hunt daid!"

One, two, three jumps, and she pointed at my foot. I bent over, moved the grass and there it was, alive and burrowed under the field duff. In spite of what Milt asked, I broke his commandment and spoke to the little dog. She didn't mind and even gave me the quail.

The second day was better than the first. We had the opportunity to hunt more small farms. If a wildlife artist painted them and the quail we flushed from yellow banks of wild mustard plants, he would be scoffed at for including too much. After all, true wildlife art should have just so many cabins with smoke coming out the chimney and deer standing along the lake. Maybe what we saw was a cliche, but it was a real one.

The best was saved for last. It was a huge parcel, far more than our little squad could cover, so we hit just a couple of high spots. Milt put four dogs on the ground: they were all pointers, and they were all business. It was quiet for over an hour. We skirted the sand-bur hills and crossed dry creek bottoms, but we had no points.

Dennis and I had most of a limit by then, though I was still three shy of the legal ten birds. The return swing put us within a hundred yards of the Chevy Suburban where we had started. That's where the birds had been all the time. Dennis and Milt had a point. They walked in, and a covey came up that challenged my ability to count in clumps. They came my way.

I shucked and shot the Model 12 three times.

"My Lawd," said Aaron, "you got a triple!"

We couldn't find the last one. Milt walked back to the trailer, opened all of the doors, and covered the earth with bird dogs. "We'll find it now!" he declared.

The little black-and-white setter came up with the bird. It took awhile and was great fun. There was a dog going in every direction, and some of them were actually hunting dead. The others were looking for more quail. I don't think such a free-for-all happens often in quail hunting, and there are good reasons why it shouldn't. But I think on special occasions—like taking a triple—every living thing ought to dance a little. I know I did.

Things are never what they seem to be. For the last five years, I had thought the tradition of quail shooting was gone forever. Maybe it is in some places, but in Oklahoma, the land of red dust and ragweed, there's still a way to make it happen.

Chapter Fifteen

By the Book

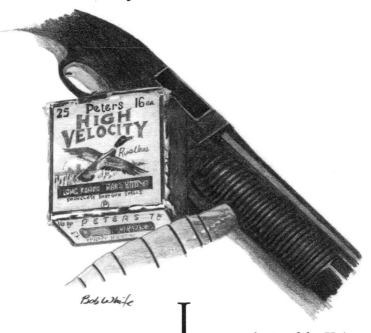

Bob White

I was a graduate of the University of Minnesota School of Law, and I had the paper to prove it. In fact, I had shelves of paper, reams of it. In about a month, I had to take the bar exam, so I rented a small room in the stacks of Walter Library. My job was to review everything that I had studied in law school so that I could spend two eight-hour days writing an essay answer to each of a series of questions to prove that I had learned something in my three years as a law student.

I was faced with the fear of failure, and the cure for fear is boredom. After three weeks of Torts and Contracts and, especially, Tax, I was bored to distraction. I wandered the narrow aisles, scanning the thousands of book bindings and brooding about the shape of things to come. A cartoon came to mind: Two rumpled lawyers are bent over a pile of manuscripts and surrounded by floor-to-ceiling shelves of heavy sheepskin-bound legal volumes. One of the lawyers says, "The answer is right here, Harry, staring us in the face."

And it was. *The Shotgunner* by Bob Nichols was a small, dark-covered book from the editor of *Sports Afield*, circa 1947. "I believe I have found something that I can understand," I said and lifted the book from the shelf. At those times, when the weighty words of McPherson vs. Buick, *res ipsa loquitor*, and the Rule Against Perpetuities stumped my ability to understand them, I turned to Nichols for guidance. In clear simple prose, he explained the best features of the best guns. It was the stuff I really needed.

I took the bar exam. Then I took a bottle of Makers Mark bourbon, sat in a chair next to my soon-to-be-former classmates, and tied on a monumental, legendary drunk. Most of us were old soldiers, and we knew how to go about it. Gathering my wits and a few hundred dollars, I took Bob Nichols's advice and bought a Model 31 Remington 12-gauge pump shotgun—the gun with the "ball-bearing action" last made in 1949. Cast from aircraft-grade aluminum, it had a twenty-six-inch improved cylinder barrel with a ventilated rib and weighed six and a half pounds, The Model 31 was the answer to the most important bar exam question: what are you going to hunt with? I already knew what I was going to be doing to earn a living, at least between bird seasons.

Until I bought my first Model 31, my only shotgun was a Remington Model 29. Common sense tells us that it must be the predecessor to the Model 31, but that is the only sense that can carry us very far. The Model 29 was as long as a Sunday-school sermon and twice as weighty; plus, it loaded and ejected from the bottom, and sometimes did both things at once.

The Model 31 came on the market as a smoother-sliding, improved design to compete with the Winchester Model 12. Remington's problem was that the Model 12 had them lapped on the market racetrack by nineteen years. Over time, I bought four Model 31s and five barrels that were choked from skeet to trap full; all of them had ventilated ribs. I picked up a Model 31 action for spare parts, along with another barrel that I cut to twenty-four inches and equipped with a Poly Choke.

The crown jewel of the Model's group is the 31 TC, the trap competition design. I am not a world-class trapshooter, and I won't become one: I can't bend my brain to the single-minded purpose that trapshooting requires. Somewhere in the race to break two hundred clay birds, my eye-to-hand nerve endings cry out for a rest. My mind takes a vacation, and I miss. My gun is fully capable of the work—as a conservative guess, I have run twenty-five thousand shells through her—but the gunner is weak. She is a rare sight on today's range, which is why I have never bought another target gun: My old Model 31 is an invitation for shotgunners to say, "Hey that's a 31 TC; I had one of those." And a story follows.

"It's a great gun," an old guy once said to me. "I don't know why I sold mine. The only trouble it ever gave me was the breech end of the slide bar snapped off."

Sometimes old trapshooters can be prophets. During one shoot, on the 175th target, the slide-bar end snapped from my Model 31 TC. I went to my parts action, salvaged the slide mechanism from it, and got back into business.

The first fine bird gun that I ever handled was a W.C. Scott & Sons side-by-side made in Birmingham, England, at the turn of the century. Picking up such a fine gun, whether this make or another, will alter your nerve endings forever. These firearms are the designer-made addictive drug of the gun world. It made me look for a twin.

A Parker side-by-side 12 gauge was as close as I could come. Mine was a little overweight in the middle, like most Americans, but it handled like the Scott. The barrels had been honed until their patterns were perfect side-to-side ovals. I never measured the chokes; I just killed grouse. I killed birds that I shot behind and those that I shot too far ahead of. They all fell stone dead. In one season, over one hundred grouse—including three doubles—fell to the Parker.

On the downside, the Parker was heavy. A 20-gauge side-by-side started to look attractive. I had taken a few detours with 20-gauge guns. There was a short-barreled Spanish AyA that went away after I missed a looping gimme that barely cleared the brush tops. I had a Browning over-and-under 20-gauge Lightning that didn't work for me at all; indeed, I would have needed two shells to commit suicide. The best I can say about the Browning is that its ejectors were spectacular. There were others, but each of these shotguns was a small step to the top—a Westley Richards 20-gauge side-by-side with a straight grip, an open bore, and a feathery weight of five and one-quarter pounds. When I took the gun from its wrappings and assembled it, I realized that all that had gone before was to train me for this moment.

There are trap guns, skeet guns, duck guns, turkey guns, and goose guns—all tools for specific purposes. Then there is the Westley Richards 20-gauge grouse gun, with its catalog of the finest gun makers in England printed on the top and flats of her barrels.

Mine was built in 1898 as one of a pair and bears the number "2" on her top lever. The company records shared with me by Simon Clode, an affable and tolerant representative of the maker, proved that her original barrels were Damascus steel. In 1921, some owner in her family tree had new barrels put on by Frederick Beezley, formerly of Purdeys of London. She was reproofed in the 1950s for two-and-three-quarter-inch chambers, and her chokes were opened to four points of constriction in the right and eight in the left.

She had evolved like a bird dog at season's end—all sinew and bone and lean muscle, scratched and cut, muzzle worn down to skin, and carrying no extra weight. What remained was focused on the single purpose of finding and bringing down the king of game birds: the ruffed grouse.

Since she came to me, the Westley Richards and I have walked hand in hand through the stickery places where grouse grow. Is she the best? If not, she is close enough and compares very favorably to the best. I know, because I have handled, carried, and fired the holy grail of 20-gauge side-by-sides—the Boss sidelock double 20 gauge. Some will argue with that opinion, but if there are differences between a Boss gun and whatever is next to it, they are differences in degree, taste, and personal decoration. There can be no serious quarrel with the workmanship or design of a Boss.

Ben Moore is a friend of Steve Schneider, a man we shall meet and hear more of in later chapters. Ben owns a Boss 20-gauge side-by-side. He is much too young and vital for such a responsibility because this gun was made during the golden age of Boss craftsmanship, years before he was born. His grandfather, also named Ben, was the original owner. Ben told me this as he pointed out that the initials tooled into the gun's age-darkened and oil-stained oak-and-leather case are the same as his. When he placed the case on Steve's oak table, I had the keen surge of anticipation that the man who discovered the Dead Sea Scrolls must have felt. I was about to have a religious experience.

"Would you like to see it?" Ben asked.

Would I? I'd crawl through seventy yards of flaming buffalo dung just to touch the bumper of the car that hauled it.

"Oh, yes, I think so," I replied, quietly coughing. "I'd like that very much."

He unhitched the belts, tripped the latch, and there she was— Cleopatra unrolled from Caesar's rug. Boss made just one grade of shotgun, and it was the finest in the world. I had thought that if the gods were generous, some day I might touch a Boss 12 gauge. I was sure that I would never handle a 20-gauge Boss of any sort, let alone one that was cased in dark wood, accompanied by small, tarnished oil bottles, and with its lock, stock, and barrels in perfect harmony.

"Go ahead," Ben told me, "put it together."

I hope that he didn't hear the little whine from the back of my throat. "Thanks, I'd like to do that."

When I hesitated, Ben smiled and said, "My grandmother used it to shoot quail in Florida. Once I saw her walk back to her horse and thrust it into a saddle scabbard. I said, 'Grandma, if you do that, the bluing will wear off the muzzles.' She said, 'Ben, for heaven's sake, it's just a gun!'"

Ben's tale aside, I wondered if I should find some gloves. No, I thought, I can do this. I unlatched the forend from barrels that were twenty-six inches of flawless steel. With my right hand, I picked up the breech and fitted it to the barrels, holding the top lever to the right, then closing it slowly to lock the pieces together. I slipped the forend back against the hinge and pressed it up against the barrel lug. There was a solid "Click," and the gun was whole.

The straight-gripped stock inside my fingers felt like the foreleg of my little English setter—enough bone and muscle to run all day.

"I could hit something with this," I said, bringing the Boss to my cheek .

"Well, you'll have a chance," Ben Moore said. And he was good to his word: he let me carry the Boss that afternoon at our preserve pheasant hunt. I handed him my 12-gauge side-by-side, and for an hour I fondled the finest of bird guns.

Of course, the first thing I did at home was to pick up my Westley Richards. She felt just fine. There were differences, but only in degree. So be it. After all, grouse hunting is an unrefined pastime.

Grouse shooting suffers from natural, periodic declines of the bird population. Like the ebb and flow of the tide, bird numbers rise to heady peaks and drop into deep canyons. When the last decline arrived in Minnesota, I took to the prairies in search of sharp-tailed grouse. I carried a 12-gauge side-by-side, now an AyA No. 2, and my Model 12 Winchester in 16 gauge. The Winchester would become my favorite prairie gun. It had enough power to reach the farthest flush, and I could wrap my hand around the breech to carry it comfortably in a mile-eating, one-handed grip. I blame the intensity of the prairie sun on a normally tree-shaded brain for the idea that was born next. I decided that the answer to bird hunting must be a 16-gauge double. I studied the matter, turning pages in books and magazines, until I had the specifications for the ideal upland-bird killer.

Within a month a package arrived, and in it was an AyA Model 453 boxlock 16 gauge with case-colored action, straight-grip stock, and barrels of exactly twenty-seven and one-half inches bored skeet on the right and light modified on the left. The Deep Portage Chapter of the Ruffed Grouse Society—all four of us—meets on Mondays at our favorite sporting-clays range. Among the group is Norm Moody, the same fellow who likes to take naps after lunch and to declare hunting trails off-limits to all-terrain vehicles. He has one other habit. Any missed clay is followed by a declaration that the gun in use should be donated to the society's annual banquet. I didn't miss many clays with the AyA 16-gauge double: it was a killer. My idea had been proven by the facts, and the prairie birds were about to suffer.

Pride is a flower, says James Howell, that grows in the devil's garden. The 16-gauge AyA would not kill birds, at least not in my hands. I fired it at sharptails flushing from points, from tree rows, and from hilltops. The only birds I killed with it were from a group of Hungarian partridge, but I didn't flush another covey during the entire hunt. On my return home, I took it grouse hunting. On the edge of a pasture, Beans pointed a grouse that came up and climbed instead of bending one way or the other. I missed the bird twice. The gun was good as gone that day.

Over coffee, I told Norm about my troubles and said that he should take the AyA with him to South Dakota on his prairie chicken hunt. He agreed. "I'll let you know how I do," he said.

The phone rang the following Tuesday. I was muddling through a complex land title and was not happy about it. "It's Norm Moody," said my secretary. "He wants to talk to you about something."

"What thing?" I asked her. My secretaries never let anyone use generalities. One is a native German, and the other manages a cattle ranch.

"He said he wants to talk to you about Theodore."

I picked up the phone. "Who's Theodore?"

"Your old gun," he said. "I named it."

"I called it a few things but never that."

"I am standing out here on the prairie, and I have killed nine consecutive birds; a combination of pheasants and prairie chickens and sharptails. I shot them all with Theodore."

"I'll make you a helluva deal on that gun," I said.

"I know you will. Otherwise, I'll tell the world."

I admit that with the possible exception of a bolt-action goose gun with a forty-inch barrel, I have never seen a shotgun that I didn't love. The only time I have gotten into trouble is when I allowed my brain to get in the way of my muscle memory. Pumps, automatics, side-by-sides, and over-and-unders—I am helpless when faced with them. As the hand follows the eye, when I pick up a shotgun that I like, it is going home with me. You can make book on it.

Bob White

Chapter Sixteen

A School of Thought

Labrador retriever is God's thought taken form. Because I have known some Labs in my time, and if they truly reflect God's thoughts, I have sometimes wondered what in the world was He thinking?

Labradors, and retrievers in general, are easy to connect to a loving and giving God. I have owned and trained two Labs in my life. Dixie was the first, and except for an addiction to eating garbage, she never formed a malicious thought in her life. I accepted her adoration; it was endless. In her brown eyes, the fact that I had risen in the morning was a miracle, and all else in the day was continuing confirmation that I was wonderful. I trained her, but really all I did was restrict the pure instincts already in place to certain times and places: Sit, Stay, Come, and Back. The last command was my signal to get whatever I had thrown, shot, or lost. I have told this story before, but it bears repeating as an example of her incredible tolerance of my poor judgment

There is a corner on top of a green hill. It is formed by the intersection of two trails and, because it is in the sunlight, a thick growth of aspen whips and brush. By previous experience, I knew that a covey of grouse had adopted that place as their fall home. It was as close to a guarantee of a grouse flush as a bird hunter is allowed. My dark-haired bride—my new wife, not Dixie—was my companion on that sunny afternoon. Of course, I wanted to deepen her admiration of my prowess (a line of thought I have since abandoned).

In those days it was just the three of us, a trinity of sorts: man, wife, and retriever.

I had planned it well. We avoided the easy walk up the trail and slipped in from the side. When we stepped out of the brush the grouse were right under Dixie's nose. Not just one or two birds, but an even dozen. Two coveys had gathered to crop the clover, and they rose in a thunder.

"Shoot!, Shoot!" I yelled at Cheryl, then took the first of the group, dropping it on the trail. I missed the second shot, but with the speed that the Remington Model 31 allowed me, took a third shot and bounced another bird. It coasted across the trail and downhill into the heavy trees below. "Back! Back!" I hollered to Dixie.

I turned to look at Cheryl. She was standing quite still, with her eyes wide and her mouth slightly open. The shotgun remained at a slack-armed rest. "Wow!" she said, "Did you see all those partridge?"

I looked up the trail, and there stood Dixie, tail swinging happily, with the first bird in her mouth. All I could think of was the one that got away. Gesturing toward the trees, I yelled "Back!" two or three more times, then marched off in that direction, looking, I suppose, like a canvas-clad drum major.

I puffed and fussed around in the trees, and in a little while—though not nearly soon enough to suit me—Dixie came down and joined me. She appeared sad, and she did not have the first bird.

"Oh, great, just great," I whined. "Now I have lost two birds instead of one."

Fuming my way up hill, I came out on the trail and complained loudly about fate not delivering the perfect ending to my perfect ambush. Poor Dixie; she followed along with her ears and tail down and eyes cast to the ground.

"I lost the second bird," I said to Cheryl. "And to make matters worse, Dixie lost the first one." Dixie seemed to agree that she was to blame for all of it.

"Ted, for heaven's sake," Cheryl replied in a tone that I would hear many times in later years, usually in connection with the discipline of children, "Dixie dropped the first bird in the middle of the trail and came down to see you. It's right there. Honestly, you get so upset."

"Oh," I replied in a suitably quiet voice. Now both Dixie and I had our ears and tails down. God and Cheryl had spoken.

The other black Labrador was Jet. Dixie was so filled with the capacity for love that she had enough left over to raise my English setter pup, Salty. They became so bonded that it was common to see them together on a winter afternoon on the sunny side of my garage. Salty, almost pure white, would be laying on top of Dixie and taking full advantage of her black-fur thermal collector. Jet, on the other hand, was somewhat less than Dixie in every department except retrieving. She was like some professional athletes, wonderful when working but otherwise impossible to live with. If Jet was divine thought taken form, then it was from the mind of a lesser god.

She had a hard game for her first five years. Duck hunting was so bad that I took a leave of absence from the sport. Jet became Salty's assistant, the minister of retrieving grouse. I don't know if a dog can suffer from an inferiority complex, but Jet knew her place in the pack, and it was never, ever, in front of the white setter.

I sent two Wisconsin hunters into a large, state-managed tract of land lying south of a well-known duck lake. They had asked me for a tip, and, though I had never been in there myself, I allowed that there might be some woodcock and grouse in the clear-cut. Please let me know how it works out, I told them. They came back full of praise, which distressed me a bit, and a tip on a small lake in the middle of the management area. They had found it covered with mallards. I reviewed a topographical map, and, sure enough, there was the lake with the number "1314" printed in the middle and denoting its elevation above sea level.

A Bird in the Hand

It looked to me as if Lake 1314 deserved some attention, and Jet deserved her first duck hunt. I drove out in the late afternoon, found a place to park off the trail, and walked to the lake, which was actually a small, kidney-bean-shaped puddle in the bottom of a steep-sided bowl. I planned for an early morning return, so I made a few landmarks to help me find it in the dark.

It's not fun to walk through dog-hair poplar in chest waders at any time, particularly so when toting a shotgun and a sack of decoys in the dark of morning. However, the beaver channel between the shore and the house was at least waist deep, and walking in waders is easier than dragging a boat.

There were no ducks on the lake, but I found a beaver house dug into the bog. I thought that I could use it to watch the sun rise, but beaver houses are impossible to perch on. Your toes are either headed uphill or downhill. At first I sat on the house; then I stood up; finally, I laid down. Jet took up a spot on the front side and waited. The day was going to be clear, utterly cloud free. When the early light was about to shift into full sunrise, there were only two colors: a yellow sky that tinted the water, and a black band where the trees and shoreline met the yellowish lake. There wasn't a breath of wind.

I heard the first flock but did not see them land. They came into the lake from the north and dropped in without circling. The ripples moved the yellow-hued water, and I could see the flock was a nice bunch of black-and-white divers. Then another bunch came in behind the first. These were followed by a third flock— again, all bluebills—numbering well over one hundred. I rolled over onto my back and watched flock after flock of ducks stack up over the little lake before pitching in. They were filling the open water. Some even hovered just above other ducks, then dropped a foot or two to splash in.

At one point, the wing noise was a thrumming, whishing pulse. I think every diver in northern Minnesota had picked that puddle of a lake to land in. Flocks swam past my beaver house, but most of them—eventually, all of them—put their heads under their wings and went to sleep. It was time to shoot. It had been five years of no duck hunting, and I had been delivered into the mother lode.

I did not shoot. To disturb what was in front of me, for ten seconds of action and a couple of ducks, would have been a breach of faith. If that thought is lost on you, then I happily confess to being a fool. What had happened to me? I had the sense to recognize a once-in-a-lifetime event and the brains to leave it alone. For the next hour and a half, I lay on my belly peaking over the top of the mound and taking in a carpet of bluebills. They were probably a raft of ducks that lifted off together from the big lake up north and flew all night, spreading themselves across the sky by speed and custom, until the leader took them down to this spot.

I looked at my watch. The ducks were waking up, and Jet was getting restless. "Time to go, black dog," I said and stood up. If you have ever seen those domino-stacking championships on television, you can appreciate what happened next. The birds nearest to me (ten feet) startled up, and the surprise spread across the pond. Picture a huge, thin rug being picked up by one edge and shaken. Thousands of ducks were getting the message that said "fly for your lives!" I was in the middle of a swirling tornado of black-and-white birds.

I set my shotgun on the edge of the beaver house and picked up my decoys, one at a time, wading in the moat around the stick-covered cone. Jet stood on the top and gave me one of those head-cocked, ears-up, question-mark looks.

"That's right new dog, I am exactly who you think I am—an old guy whose idea of fun has changed." On the other hand, I saw four wood ducks beating along the shore in a loose bunch, flying below all of the other traffic. I picked up my Remington and waited patiently. They crossed over our corner, and I selected a drake from the group. A shot, a drop, and a splash.

"Back!" I commanded, and Jet retrieved her first duck. She seemed to enjoy the work, so I let her carry the bird all the way to the truck. Jet was less than old Dixie, but it wasn't her fault. Some dogs with a God-given gift don't get a chance to play the game. All retrievers share that purity of function. They find the bird, grab it, and bring it back. They are hardwired by their instincts and have the privilege of doing the thing that God put them on earth to do, usually with minimal interference from man. There are exceptions to the rule, of course; the most notable being the pointing Labrador. But I put that down to man meddling with a biddable disposition by breeding for canine indecision. In conformance with the divine plan, instinct drives the predator to grab the prey. Anything short of that is called "pointing." In order to make it happen, man had to get involved and create a different animal.

Pointing dogs are man's thought taken form. And it's a good thought. Generations of selective breeding have created a nose, carried by four legs, that stops short of frightening the prey and causing it to fly away. In the meantime, the hunter comes swiftly or slowly, depending on the prey, and flushes it so that it can be killed. The dog runs to pick it up and brings it back to the hunter, uneaten. That's the thought as formed by man. The execution of the thought and the form of the dog are variations on the same theme. Think of pointers, setters, shorthairs, and even Brittanies as keys of a piano, each playing a single note of the pointing-dog symphony.

The cleanest, hardest steel edge of man's thought is the pointer. It is the racecar of the bird-finding game boiled down to nose and muscle. The first one I saw was at a field trail. I don't know if that pointer was good or bad, because the contest was local, but the dog covered ground with a single purpose. To those hapless, penraised quail, it was the wrath of God. The next pointer that I met was Ruby, the liver-and-white lady of Dale Spartas. In the woods she was a racecar in an off-road game, but given any amount of space, particularly islands of aspen in a pasture, Ruby would flat get it done! Watching her in comparison to my two German short-hairs, I was reminded of a story about Pablo Picasso. His fellow artists would hide their paintings from him—if he saw an original idea he would go home and in a day paint everything there was to paint in that genre. Milt Rose, my Oklahoma guide, ran pointers because they were an extension of his passion to find wild quail. If a dog did not produce, it would not be in Milt's trailer for long. Pointers are like that: they are a weapon. I don't want to own one because I spend too much time in tight covers. But I would like to have a pointer in powdered form that I could shake onto the ground, pour water on top of it, and let it rip across the prairie.

Setters are softer than pointers. A bird hunter can love a setter, and the dog will love him back. Setters are lovely and inspire long, romantic names. You never hear of a setter named Spike. I named my girl Salty after her white color, but for the first two years of her life, I added some descriptive profanity to her name. She developed rather slowly; one might say her speed exceeded her brakes. I worked hard to exert my will upon her, and she worked hard to dodge out of its way. One bright afternoon, in the presence of two witnesses, she busted five grouse out of a corner. Then, seeing how much fun that was, she barreled back down the trail at warp speed only to trip over a grouse hunkered in the grass, rolling the bird over at least once. As she dug her feet under her, the bird regained its balance and flew off. She watched it go, then trotted back to me, flopped on her side, panting, and waited for the consequences. I could not form words. Mostly, I spit foam.

Salty had the fortune of putting her game together at the peak of the grouse cycle. She also had that rarest of instincts—the genetic splice for handling ruffed grouse. Somewhere in her long line, a coupling took place that combined just the right amount of restraint with the same amount of choke-bore nose. I have watched her work open ground under gray-dogwood bushes. Her tireless rocking-chair lope would condense, suddenly, into an egg-walking creep, then into a hard point. Out in front of her stood a grouse, an unmistakable brown triangle with a bobbing head. When it moved, she moved, and the bird would freeze in place. Even when the grouse could see me coming, it was reluctant to run. She hypnotized them. That's why I kept my Labradors—if I had hunted Salty by herself, I would have needed only a sack. Well, perhaps that is an exaggeration, but the Lab (with Salty's permission) would dive in and, if my part was true, bring back the victim.

I wouldn't want to say that Spence Turner lost the genetic link, but after Salty (she was out of Spence's Samantha) passed on I got another English setter from him. This was Dots, a canine comet with lean, rippling muscles and a chiseled, predatory head. She was an intoxication to own. When I trained her in the field next to my house, cars stopped and passengers stared at the way she moved across the ground. But she was too much dog for my game.

Spence thought that a male from the same litter, a dog named Smith, would be about right. I had come down to Missouri for my annual quail-hunting trip and for the first time had no dog.

"Try him out," Spence said. "He's not as wide as Dots, but he has a good nose."

He was also a hungry dog. Smith and I worked the edge of a creek that wound around a crop field. I startled up two quail and killed the pair, putting one on the land and the other into the creek, where it floated like a huge trout fly. Smith rose to the bait. He waded into the stream and scooped up the quail, then stood in the water looking at me. Tom Kuschel walked over. We both stared at Smith, and he stared back.

I opened my double, caught the empties, and pushed the dry-land quail into my vest. "He's thinking about something," I said to Tom.

"Yeah," he replied. "He's thinking about breakfast."

"Do you suppose?" I asked.

Smith answered. The quail bobbed up and down, then in a gulp the bird was gone. Smith walked out of the stream, shook off the water, looked back for a moment, and trotted off.

"I believe that Smith just told me to get off the setter wagon."

It was good advice, though I never got a chance to thank him properly. Another dog had adopted me for the remainder of the hunt. Like all good German shorthairs, she worried about me. Over the next three days, if I lost a quail and was kicking around in the grass, a brown face would appear. Josie was on the job. If other dogs pointed, Josie would back them. No fallen quail escaped her. Josie was a walking-hunter's dream.

Her owner was Tim Schrage, the son-in-law of Dave Mackey. "Tim, have you ever had Josie bred?" I asked.

"Yes, she had a litter this year," he said.

"They're all gone, I suppose."

"No," he said, "I heard about your troubles, so I kept out a male. Do you want to see him?"

"Lead me to the kennel."

Tim got ahead of me and opened the door of the shed. A gray-and-liver pup walked out, stretched, turned in my direction, and then at a hard run crossed the lawn and jumped into my arms. I was adopted into the world of the versatile hunting dog.

"Well, I suppose that will be all right," said Spence, when I thanked him for the opportunity to own Smith but passed on it. "You're in it for the kill, not the dog work."

The pup became Beans. My wife already had a lap dog named Porky, and I thought the two names went together nicely. Later I bought a female shorthair and named her Bisquit. She didn't work out, so I bred Beans to a lovely female that produced an irresistible, white-bodied, brown-headed baby boy that I wanted to name Gravy.

"No!" Cheryl said, "that's enough with the food names. Pick something simple."

The son of Beans became Butch. As a concession to his heritage, I wrote the name out as "Buch."

Shorthairs are where I am at. They develop quickly, and most important, they worry about me. Salty let me hunt with her. Sometimes she would check back to see what was keeping me, but, mostly, my job was to find her. Beans and Butch come back to see if I need anything. If they had a cold beer, it would be mine. They think their function on earth is to take care of me and provide me with whatever it is I ask of them. If I don't ask them to do something, they find an object of interest to bring to me.

One time they were chased back to me by a black bear, another time it was a timber wolf. Butch once found two snarling otters—the smallest of the two, about the size of a big cat, backed both shorthairs down the trail and into the water of a creek before swimming off. I have killed seven skunks (but not before five of them sprayed Beans) with my highborn Westley Richards, a record, I think, for a gun of that impeccable breeding. Butch has notched up a coyote and a porcupine.

They don't wear bells or beepers. Beans loves to hunt ducks and will sit in a blind with a rapt attention turned to the sky. Butch loves to hunt pheasants and herds them like a cutting horse.

My shorthairs are the pickup trucks of the pointing-dog world. They start reliably every morning, do their work without fanfare, and retire at night. If they could clean the guns and cook, I think they would.

Over the years, I have been instructed by the best in the bird-hunting business, my dogs. The purpose of my education has been to find birds. I provide the transportation and the food, they provide the reason we are out there. I'm not in it for the dog work, that's too one-sided. I'm in it for the bird work. After all, a dog without a bird is just a dog.

BobWhite

Chapter Seventeen

The Gift

Sometimes you have to give yourself what you wish you could get from someone else. I had made up my mind that for the first time in years no one was going to help me kill the few grouse I had located on land that I had begged. My Missouri quail hunts were done for, and I had no contacts or acquaintances that I could pester for pheasants. A splendid fall lay before me, but with the prospect of a mediocre grouse season, I needed a bird-hunting trip. I wanted to strike off in a new direction during this downtime, to go west to the prairie and experience the elements of grassland bird hunting without the distraction of other people's needs or expectations.

The venerable membership of the Deep Portage Chapter of the Ruffed Grouse Society had closed out the summer's clay shooting, wrapped up the annual banquet, and were already on the hills and buttes of North Dakota. While Beans and I sweated our way through the early season green, those privileged few were running their setters in the prairie sun, breathing free, and walking with long strides. Sharp-tailed grouse were flushing and falling.

But I had one tip: the name of a North Dakota wildlife management area. Given my experience with Missouri management areas, I had little reason for optimism. I could add to that my two sharptail-hunting adventures in northwestern Minnesota. Both ended in a skunking—a birdless one for me, and a real one for the dog. I had lots of reasons to stay home, which is why I packed the pickup, put Beans in the cab, and headed west.

I had reservations at a motel in Harvey, North Dakota, one that didn't mind a hunting dog sharing the room. I had no other reservations or expectations. A little basic knowledge passed along by the Deep Portage Venerables covered two points: (1) if the grass is too thick to see your boots, you are hunting in the wrong place; and (2) sharptails like hills and are usually found just under the top on the leeward side.

It was September on the prairie, one week after the sharptail opener, and the state of North Dakota lay before me, open for exploration. The most important thing was to get off the interstate and onto the two-lane highways. I crossed the Red River and, leaving Fargo and the national-chain restaurants behind me, turned into Buffalo, where I stopped at Clem and Hazel's Corner Cafe. I looked at the locals, and they looked at me. Hazel had made meat loaf for the dinner special that came complete with a slice of cake. The bill was written on a stiff piece of heavy paper with the corner turned under. I paid it and, being curious, asked my waitress about the check.

"Why's the corner of this turned under? I said, pushing it smooth.

"So's you can pick it up easy," she said.

The east side of North Dakota is flat, suitable for travel and agriculture. Once you get out of the Red River Valley, the next change in the land happens along the edge of the Missouri Coteau. This region is as close to diverse topography as the middle of North Dakota gets. The Coteau is a slanted line of potholes and hills stretching from the north side of the state and running on into its neighboring Dakota to the south. U.S. Route 52 is pretty much the line that describes the Coteau's edge. I turned at Jamestown, passing up a chance to see the world's largest buffalo, and set my tires in the northbound lane of Route 52. Tall plumes of smoke from fires were everywhere. Later on this trip, I would learn that it is a common practice to burn the chaff left from the wheat harvest, but at this stage in my prairie career I did not know what wheat chaff looked like. The Venerables had talked about flushing sharptails from wheat stubble. I was driving past miles and miles of it but had no idea what it was. I knew corn, beans, and sunflowers. Wheat was the tall, golden grass that rippled in the wind and was bound into sheaves. Let's not even get into snowberries, buffalo berries, and prairie rose hips. At this point, I was delighted to see to the edge of tomorrow.

There are some things in North Dakota that you can't see. If you stand on the edge of the Harvey Hornet's practice field watching them get ready for the big game against Carrington, don't wear a yellow shirt and stand next to a white pickup. If you do, your skin will begin to burn and itch. It isn't the sun; it's a bug. If you look very carefully and closely at the door and side of the truck, you will see that it is covered with tiny, black specks. Switch your gaze to your own shirt, and you will see that you are covered as well.

I turned to a nearby native and asked, "What have I got all over me?"

"Uhmmm, sunflower gnats," he said. "They love white and yellow."

"What are they?" I replied, sweeping my hands over my arms and neck.

"Oh, sorta North Dakota's answer to the Canadian bug called a no-see-um."

"Man, they itch like fire!" I said.

"Oh yeah, they're real fond of people. Wherever you got sunflowers, you got gnats," he said and returned to the practice. "That's why we play football at night."

There's one other thing in Harvey. At about 5 A.M., I woke up to the sound of a diesel truck traveling along the street. Then it came back. Shortly, it returned the same way. This continued, back and forth, until I finally got up, opened the door, and looked out. It wasn't a truck; it was a train engine shifting cars from one place to another. (Trains left my part of the country a long time ago.) Beans was up, and I was excited to get going.

I had driven to the Lone Tree Wildlife Management Area after my gnat attack the day before. There is a headquarters more or less in the middle of the world's largest collection of overgrown fencerows and windbreaks. The country has the appearance of a place where farming came to a halt, then began again with haphazard fits and starts. And that's pretty much what happened. The Lone Tree was originally supposed to be underwater after the land was purchased for the Garrison Dam diversion of the Missouri River. Apparently, the government bought more land than they needed. That was good news for wildlife. It turned out to be good news for me, too, because I met Scott Peterson, the biologist in charge of the area.

Scott Peterson is the guy you would like to have come to the door when you picture yourself driving into a perfect farm to ask permission to hunt. You know what I mean; the ideal landowner who is happy to see you and says of course you can hunt, don't forget to come back for coffee, and you don't have to ask permission the next time. Scott even gave me a map, on which he circled the latest sharptail information collected by his field staff. Damn good luck for a guy who still doesn't know wheat stubble from crabgrass. The truth be known, in the Lone Tree wheat stubble isn't a big item. What matters is reclaimed native prairie, potholes, blown-down windbreaks, and old farmsteads. The walking will be the same as it was a century ago.

One other thing had not changed—the wind. One time in Missouri, Tom Kuschel and I hunted quail in the fields below the house on Fairview Farm. The wind was blowing so hard that we could not carry on a conversation. I climbed a hill and out of the corner of my eye I could see a gust coming across the switch-grass below us.

"Tom!" I hollered. "Watch this." I stood still, facing toward the wave of wind as it flattened the grass and roared up the hill. Spreading my arms, with my shotgun in one hand, I leaned out just as it came upon us. It held me, strong and steady, though I was angled out so far that I should have fallen. That evening, the weatherman reported wind gusts in excess of fifty miles an hour. The quail would flush into the gale and hang there for a moment until, "like leaves that before the wild hurricane fly," they were blown past us.

The wind was my partner on my first day of sharptail hunting in North Dakota.

I couldn't sense its strength in town. The Venerables had said that the best plan was to be on the road by first light.

"Drive slow and watch for birds returning from feeding," they said. "When you see them, mark them down, then walk them up." I take instruction well. Beans and I puttered along in the Ford, looking to the left and right for anything. I saw tumbleweeds and leaves and shards of grass but nary a feathered creature. We came to a line of ridges, one after the other, above a dry creek bottom that Scott had marked as a likely location. I stopped. It was time to put our feet on the ground. I reached for the door handle.

"I'm going to stand on the doorsill and look down the draw," I announced to Beans. He was neutral on the idea. I opened the door, raised my head above the cab, and my cap was gone. "Whuff!" Just like that. The door came back against me, and I was caught like a stick in a clam. Welcome to North Dakota.

I retrieved my cap—though I had to chase it down—then I found a parking spot out of the wind. However, I did not find any sharptails. The birds definitely didn't love the lee side of the creek-bed ridges, and it had been a hunt of a mile and a half each way. A long walk for nothing, but a good walk. Instead of starting and stopping, turning to go around deadfalls and stepping over fallen logs, the walk had been a strong stride over short grass. Beans loved it. He made long casts, then, feeling guilty, he would turn to come back, but the boss was in plain view. In North Dakota, everything is plain view.

According to my map, there was a sharptail dancing ground up the road, at the end of a trail on the right. A long shelterbelt of Russian olives, scattered cedars, and assorted shrubs split the flat dancing ground from a half-harvested field of sunflowers. (According to the Venerables, sharptails love sunflowers.) The windbreak shrubs were the first vertical plants above knee height that we had worked. I took the lee side, on the field edge. Beans moved in and out between the rows and was out of sight longer than he should have been. I was carrying my side-by-side 12 gauge; it had an ounce of No. 7½ shot in the improved-cylinder barrel and a one-ounce handload of No. 5 shot in the modified barrel.

I heard the most peculiar sound. It wasn't cackle or a whistle but a throaty chuckle— "Kuck, kuck, kuck"—coming right for me. Creamy-colored birds, mottled with brown specks, burst through the cedar tops like ruffed grouse. The logical side of my brain said "what's that?" while the hunter side said "shoot!"

I obeyed the hunter side and shot twice, killing the first and second sharptails of my life. Beans skidded out from under the shrubbery, hit his accelerator, and knocked the first bird back to the earth as it flopped in the sunflower field. The other grouse, struck by a tight pattern of No. 5s, was motionless on the ground. I had taken a true double, a singular event on its own but more so when combined with my first sharptail.

What a handsome bird; larger and heavier than a ruffed grouse, with broad wings and the distinctive tail that gives it its name. The sharptail had been conquered, it was only noon, and I had two-thirds of a daily limit. What was I going to do with the rest of the day?

I was going to walk. Beans and I headed to the field corner, then down the next side, along a lake, and up to the top of a butte. We sat on the high ground for awhile, taking in sunshine and looking at a twinkle of light that was probably my pickup's mirror reflecting from a row of trees. Then we hunted along the ridgetop, stepping through low-growing, gray green snowberries and clumps of black-stemmed buffalo berries. I could see an agricultural edge, a straight line cut in the prairie grass. I headed for the edge, and in an hour or so I made it.

"Hmmm," I said to Beans, "little stalks of something sticking straight up all over the field. I'm thinking we have found wheat stubble." We crunched along the field edge to a point where I could see the far side, which means the mile-away side. "If there are birds out here, I sure ought to be able to see them." I told Beans.

I was both right and wrong—I couldn't see them, but they could see me. "Kuck, kuck, kuck," I heard, and a flock of sharptails lifted off the field and flew out of sight in their distinctive flap-and-coast style.

"Well, for heaven's sake. I didn't even shoot at them. Talk about taking easy offense. Time for a rest, Beans," I said, then walked off the field and laid in the grass.

This is the best part of prairie hunting. Boots off, feet drying in the sun, and up in the sky, so very far off that they are hardly in sight, sandhill cranes turn slow circles as they are blown south. They have a voice that they can lay down on the prairie right next to you; it sounds like a bag of stones being rattled in oil. The Lone Tree is right on an ancient flight path, according to Scott, and the cranes gather in the same places as their ancestors. "Not very far south of here," he said, "right around Goodrich."

"Wake up dog." I roused Beans from his nap. "We have one more to get. Let's try the dancing ground."

The wind had eased, settling to the ground along with the sun.

A Bird in the Hand

We walked around the hilltops, down into the bottoms, and back up the sides. One man and one dog do not cut a wide swath in this land. The dancing ground had been mowed, which made for easy but unproductive walking. I had about given up hope for a last bird and was pacing along, my shotgun swinging in my right hand. I should have been paying attention to the dog, but fatigue had narrowed my view to the few square feet of ground in front of me. I almost stepped on the first of five birds that flushed.

It is uncanny how a sharptail can hide where a golf ball would be obvious. It is also unsettling. The first barrel went off, pointed somewhere. But I followed the bird, got past it, and sent the heavy No. 5s out to where the two fliers collided. Beans picked up my final third of a limit, and the day was made. I had become a prairie bird-hunter and had three sharptails and a pair of tired legs to prove it.

On the open prairie, time does not pass by; it is always right beside you. I suppose it is the lack of a comparative measure—there are no young trees growing next to old trees, and no matter where you walk, the horizon doesn't change. The light grows in the morning and dies at sunset. Whether you walk ten yards or ten miles, it is pretty much the same. There is no past and there is no future. It is a timepiece of the present. Consider floating on a lake, just letting the boat drift in the wind, so slow and easy that you drop your fishing line and bobber into the water just to be sure of movement. Now consider floating on a creek or river where there is clearly a current, a direction, a perception of movement, and two banks for guidance. The prairie is like that lake. My life back home is the river. A few more days out here and my coil might get so unwound that I won't be able to tighten up for the river traffic.

Chapter Eighteen

Turning the Corner

The room clerk left a note on my door. It seemed that a wedding party needed my space the next day. One dusty bird hunter and his tired dog don't count for a whole lot in Harvey, North Dakota. Well, they said the room was available, but they didn't say for how long.

"Beans," I said, crumpling up the paper, "there is an overbooking policy at this establishment. We are to pack our kit and be gone by midday tomorrow." I didn't expect much sympathy from a partner that spends most of his free time in the back of a pickup. "That's fine with me, because this train's alarm clock is set too early, no matter what the Venerables say."

In the morning, I intended to eat a normal breakfast at a human hour with the citizens of Harvey. I had already cleaned two of my sharptails and placed the marinading meat on ice for my lunch. I would grill it, cover the meat with my favorite barbecuing sauce, and eat the pride of the prairie under an old cottonwood tree. If I couldn't find a place to stay, no matter; there were some lovely campsites in the Lone Tree, and I had brought my sleeping bag and mattress pad. I was too mellow to care. Life had thrown me an aggravation that ordinarily would have flared my temper. Too bad for whatever little devil thought up that one. On the prairie there's room enough for everything.

The day was overcast and brooding about rain. A new front had followed its windy introduction, darkening one group of clouds over the town but leaving lighter and drier relatives to float above the Lone Tree. I returned to my shelterbelt and found their orderly lines empty. The same walk as yesterday without the good results. Nothing had changed on the hills overlooking the lake. During my foot travel between the hilltops, I had flushed ducks off the potholes and had been awestruck by the volume of waterfowl. Every variety of dabbling duck was here. Some were in such great numbers that a pothole would hold only a single species. An entire lake would be full of mallards, and next to it another brimful of teal. I wasn't becoming jaded, but I took for granted that the sky would be filled by a constant shuffle of ducks. Above them all, the sandhill cranes had a lot to say about the weather forcing them to fly at less than ten thousand feet. Even Beans, who loves ducks, shrugged them off and no longer charged into the potholes. Life on the prairie agreed with him as well. Although he extended his usual range to on the edge of "way too far," I let him hunt without interference. The landscape was enormous, he knew what we were looking for, and sharptails hold well in the early season.

It was midmorning. The rain had held off, but we were still birdless. The last stop on my circuit was going to be the dancing grounds—yesterday evening the birds had been in that area. But this was morning, and the daily habits of the sharptail remained a mystery to me. About all I could say up to this point was where the grouse were not. They were not in the shelterbelts or on the hilltops or along the waterways. All those conclusions applied only to this little square of a few miles.

I stood up, shrugged on my vest, and picked up the side-by-side 12 gauge. I liked this gun. It was an AyA sidelock with dark wood and engraved, case-colored side-plates. I had ordered it for all forms of bird hunting, except ruffed grouse. It was sort of the versatile hunting dog of shotguns because it had been fitted for screw-in choke tubes. Most important, when the bird hunting was slow, or when I was tired and walking with my head down, it was pretty to look at. Today, the gun was looking especially lovely.

The dancing grounds were south of the shelterbelt tree rows. I didn't need to toss dust in the air for wind direction—even though it was a relatively quiet day, it was still North Dakota. Beans and I climbed the plateau on the downwind side. The truck, and lunch, was a mile away. I figured the best way to cross the grassy flat was to zigzag in a wide swath and take in as much of the land as possible. We crunched along, concentrating our efforts in areas where we could see earth below the bluestem. Beans narrowed his sweep, then dropped his head, extending his nose out and level with his back. He stopped, quickstepped ahead, and stopped again.

I wasn't admiring the shotgun any more. I kept my eyes on the line between the yellow grass and the shelterbelt. I knew from my experiences yesterday that sharptails can assemble their cream-and-brown feathers from nothing more than the grass and dirt at your feet. Two came up, then one more closer to me. The near bird went down with my first shot. Then, all around me, they started to rise. I had walked into a spread-out flock of a dozen. I wasted a shot on a long, grandstand try. There was still time, if I could get the gun reloaded. The ejectors worked flawlessly. I shoved in two loads of

No. 5 shot, slapped the gun shut, and swung on a bird that had flapped long enough to start coasting.

"Back trigger, back trigger," I told myself. "Stay with it, and ride it out. That looks about right."

There was that little lag between the bang and the hit that comes with a long shot. The heavy load carried enough energy to break both of the bird's wings, and Beans saw it go down. I opened the gun and caught the empty. I love it when it comes together.

Applause drifted across the prairie. Over on the road, I saw a bright, toothy smile from a man standing next to a tractor-mower. I was right when I thought that it must be one of Scott Peterson's field crew. If there is a mold for the creation of the human to be called Son of North Dakota, the model for it was standing in front of me. He was Terry Osbourne, a sturdy, blonde, square-jawed recent graduate of North Dakota State University.

"Really?" I said. "Did you know my daughter Tessa? She went to North Dakota State and graduated in the same year." I had gone to her graduation, and I recommend that program to anyone who doubts whether America is producing and educating clean-cut, solid, smiling, and optimistic young people. They are there in the hundreds.

"Oh Yah," he answered. "Yah, Tessa, I studied with her group. Really nice gal, and really smart. Nice shot, then."

For those of you who don't know it, northwest Minnesotan and North Dakotan sentences always end by using the word "then." In Canada the word is "Ay?" It is an audible punctuation mark and a signal that it is your turn to speak. In the Midwest it is not nice to interrupt, and being nice is important.

Terry had driven up in a Chevrolet pickup. I think that one is issued to every North Dakotan, complete with a Labrador retriever. He was a treasure trove of information gained from the perspective of one who is in the Lone Tree every day. I dug out my maps, and Terry added more circles and arrows. Just at the time when I had run out my string of Lone Tree pearls, luck sent a guy to add more. My afternoon was made and ready for exploration. It was time for a sharptail lunch, and I asked Terry to join me.

"Nah," he said. "I got to get to work, then."

The cloud cover had broken into patches of blue, although there was some muttering in the west by a line of dark-blue rain carriers. It was nice enough for a tailgate lunch, a threshold just short of a snowstorm on one end and a thunderstorm on the other. I keep a grill and all the accessories stored in one of two drawers in my pickup box. The drawers are held together by a plywood deck. The dogs, decoys, coolers, and gear go on top of the deck. I keep my guns and shells in the left-hand drawer and my cooking gear, hitch parts, tow ropes, and trouble fixers in the right. A third box runs along the back of the cab, crossways to the two drawers. This is my "Oh Man" box and is where I go when I have gotten myself into a situation that forces me to say those words. Shovels, ax, saws, jacks, winches, chains, and cable live there.

The grill is a small, gas-fired model. It heated quickly, and in about twenty minutes I had cooked my marinated birds, put the meal on a slice of bread, opened a beer, and settled into my canvas chair. Life was good. It got even better when followed by a pipe, a second beer, and a nap. I woke up in the rain. It was time to find some lodging.

State Highway 200 runs straight east and west, except for one right-hand curve followed in a half mile by a left-hand curve. In between the curves is the town of Goodrich, North Dakota. I had returned to the Lone Tree headquarters for suggestions on a place to stay. Scott mentioned a new bed-and-breakfast—the Coteau Lodge—just east of Goodrich on Highway 200, and with one phone call I had a room for as long as I wanted it, together with some private farmland to hunt. First, however, I wanted to get more ice and a sandwich for supper. I pulled into Goodrich.

If North Dakota had an official hound dog, it could sleep undisturbed in the middle of Goodrich's main street. First, because there isn't much traffic; second, because the people are too nice to wake him up. I parked my truck at the post office and looked up and down the main street. From left to right, there were four store fronts—the first two were empty, the third was a cafe (closed), and the last was the grocery store. In the next block was the Goodrich Machine Co., and beyond that, the standard-issue grain elevator. I walked across the street to the store and pulled open the screen door. It creaked on its hinges exactly as it was supposed to, and when it slammed shut behind me the metal sheet advertising Wonder Bread rattled. There were ten-foot-high tin ceilings, light bulbs hanging on cords, and a floor that creaked. The tile in front of the cash register's counter was worn through to the wood. And the smell! Does every country grocery store have the wonderful scent of bread, cookies, coffee grounds, and one hundred years of trade? Maybe not. I haven't been in every one, but I once worked for Nabisco; thus, I have been in a lot of them. I would not have been surprised if the nice lady behind the counter had a muffler for a 1949 Mercury.

"Is there someplace where I can get a sandwich?" I asked.

"The cafe closes at noon, but it's almost time for Glen to open the bar. He can make you a hamburger. I'll call him up," she said. She picked up the phone and in a moment informed Glen that he had a customer and would he mind opening early? "No trouble at all," she told me. "Just go on over to the bar, and we'll be along in a bit."

I walked back across the street and hung my jacket and whistle in the truck, then looked for the sign. Every bar has a sign, or so I thought. Up the street and down the street, no sign saying "Bar." She had made it sound so close and had even gestured with her hand as if the bar (and my sandwich) was next door. The only building in the direction she had pointed was the Goodrich Machine Co., a big half-round quonset-type structure with an ice machine and a pop cooler in front. It had two doors.

I looked a bit closer, and in the window next to the left-hand door I could see a small, neon sign advertising a major brand.

"Looks like we have the Goodrich Machine Co., and Bar," I said under my breath as I walked over to try the door. It was open. A man came out of the machine-shop side wiping his hands on a rag. The gray-and-black pinstriped shirt had the name "Glen" on it. My host and chef had arrived.

"I turned on the grill when she called, but it'll take a while to heat up. What'll it be?" Glen asked.

I ordered a beer, which he picked out of the cooler, wiped clean, and opened. The room had a pool table, several smaller tables, chairs, the counter where Glen was standing, and a card table under a hanging light. I asked about the joint business.

"Well," he answered, "I like a beer after work, and so do a lot of my friends, so I walled off this part of my shop and got a liquor license. You want ketchup on the burger?"

That would be fine. After a few sips, four old men—two in bib overalls—walked in. They sat down at the card table and picked up the hands that were laying there face down. There was a brief discussion about who had the bid. One of them played a card.

"That's good," said Glen after he had delivered their cans of beer. "Yesterday that one at the end of the table threw his cards down and stomped out saying the rest of them were cheating him. Now he's back. I've seen him take two or three days to cool off." Glen slid my burger across the counter. The grocery-store crew came in and sat at a table. Nightlife in Goodrich was about to begin.

I was too tired for that much excitement, so I paid my tab, thanked Glen for his hospitality, and drove east to Coteau Lodge. The 1906 house had been towed out of Carrington and placed on a new foundation by Tim and Darcy Franz. The hunter's quarters—two bedrooms, and a main room as a gathering place—were downstairs. Because I was the only guest, I got a tour of the house. It wasn't hard to imagine a time when servants lived upstairs and ladies in ball gowns made their debut descending the main staircase. There had been some attempts at "modernization," and with Tim's help the class and quality were coming back again.

Tim and Darcy shared their farm with her folks. Their land surrounded the lodge and included a traditional stopover for sandhill cranes—cranes by the thousands. The conditions were quiet that evening, and Tim and I watched the cranes set their wings and land among their relatives. A murmur of conversation between the birds became a cheering crowd and finally a political rally. If we had wanted to talk, we couldn't have heard one another. The cranes were Tim's main asset for guiding hunters. Sharp-tailed grouse had the status of "Yah, I saw some."

I didn't need a guide, just a bed at night and land to hunt during the day. "Find some sunflowers and walk along the edge," Tim said. "The sharptails will be there." The next morning, he sent me south of the farm to an area of hilly, potholed agricultural fields. Everything I had learned about sharptails and prairie hunting didn't apply. Beans and I circled the crops and the potholes, helping the ducks stretch their wings but disturbing little else. I had uncased my Model 12 Winchester 16 gauge, which is slender and easier to carry than a side-by-side when the walking is long between birds. We paused at a hay bale. Two small hills lay between us and the next water hole.

I pointed to the nearest hill. "Beans, we'll go around the base of that one, work it back into the wind, then cross over to the other one." He gave me a look that said, "Wow, I never would've thought of that!"

It was a good plan. We were about halfway up the hillside when

Beans locked up. Straight ahead in the tall grass at the top, I could see a half-dozen sharptails alert and staring at us. "Rush 'em!" I said and took off at a run, halving the distance before they panicked and flushed. Three shots, two grouse, and a wild salute. I opened the crop of the largest bird—it was packed with grasshoppers. The sharptails weren't in the sunflowers, they were in the fields snapping up insects.

It took me most of the day to find another covey, and when I did they were on the lee side of a hilltop. All but one rose and flipped over the top out of sight. The one that chose badly coasted in a downhill flight showing its back and wings against the blue waters of a pothole. It wasn't a hard shot, but it was the prettiest I made on the trip and the one I remembered whenever I walked the cover afterward.

My first steps on the Dakota prairie happened because I gave myself what I couldn't get from someone else. I thought I wanted a bird-hunting trip. What I got was experience. In four days I had met a whole culture of friendly people, walked miles of new territory, and even shot a few birds. If I had brought a group, the trip would have been about us. Since I was alone, everything was about the new land, the small places. I could sit, then stand up and walk one hundred yards, then sit again if I felt like it. I could talk for as long as I liked to anyone I met. Because I was alone, nice people went out of their way to make me feel at home. I ate when I was hungry and slept when I was tired. Was I successful? Absolutely. Success is giving yourself the opportunity to do what you want to do. What I wanted, more than anything, was to hunt six hours without a care in the world.

Bob White

Chapter Nineteen

A Memory in Feathers

Butch—a fat, white-bodied, brown-headed pup—had been delivered one year ago. This son of Beans, born into a long line of gray-and-brown German short-haired pointers, had been different from the start. He was the undisputed king of the crowd. He was first at the dairy bar, first at the food bowl, and the first pointing dog that I had not ruled with an iron hand. Fortunately, Butch did not often test my training determination, and I had the advantage of a steady assistant coach. Beans, among his other fine qualities, was a model for Butch to follow. We worked the new boy through all the standard drills. I was optimistic: Butch was an affable, loose-jointed clone of his daddy. His first chance at wild birds, except for a brief taste of the early season grouse woods, was going to be on North Dakota sharptails. It was a good place to start. He couldn't get lost, and young sharptails are naive.

I arrived in Goodrich during the late afternoon and drove directly to a patch of prairie south of Coteau Lodge. The boys hit the ground, glad to shake off the inactivity of travel. We worked down a butte, around its edge, and into a cluster of buffalo berries, where Butch met his first deer. There was no way to train for what followed. Three does took off across the grass flats trailed at high speed by the young king.

A benefit of training with a soft hand is the permanent memory that a furious boss has on a misbehaving student. Butch had broken the most cardinal of commandments:Thou shalt not chase deer! Even better, he was caught in the act, I could make the connection, and he would remember the moment and what it was about. I let him take the deer for about a quarter of a mile. When he figured out that he could not catch whatever this new thing was, he turned around to see if his man was watching. They say that there is a statement written in Latin on the walls of certain English abbeys along the coast of the English Channel. Roughly translated, it says "Beware the fury of the Norse!" The pride of German breeding fell into the hands of an angry Norwegian.

All in all, the first little venture of the year's sharptail hunt had been a great success. Butch had learned about the sting of a leather belt applied liberally on his muscular backside. He was depressed about it for an hour, but by feeding time he had regained most of his confidence, less those small parts which were left scattered on the grasslands. If he had chased his first deer in the woods, I might never have known about it. The sharptails could wait until morning.

When I first stayed at Coteau Lodge, it was okay for a dog to be in my room, but some muddy retrievers had changed that situation. The rule, now, was that all dogs slept outside. Breakfast had been eggs, bacon, pancakes, and all manner of good things served in the kitchen. This year it was dry cereal in the main room. I happen to like dry cereal, so I was happy. A good thing, too, because the cafe in Goodrich was closed. That wasn't the only bad news. Glen, the burger-cooking mechanic of the Goodrich Machine Co., and Bar, had been killed. A car fell off its axle stands and pinned him to the floor. You can yell a lot in Goodrich, but the only thing that could wake up and come to help would have been my fictional hound dog asleep in the street. Sometimes a town can be too damn small.

The easiest place to introduce Butch to sharp-tailed grouse was the two-hill corner where the birds had been chasing grasshoppers last year. I never made it that far. A flickering of wings caught my eye as we drove the dirt road. Flying next to the passenger-side window was a sharptail. Beyond it and in front of the truck flew four more. They had flushed from a chokecherry thicket close to the road and were intent on settling into a small peninsula of prairie grass overlooking a creek bottom. I hit the brakes, thanking all the little gods for this unexpected turn of good luck. The prairie peninsula was a manageable size for one man and two dogs. More than that, I knew there were birds in it, and I knew more or less where they had flown. The youngster, Butch, would have a chance for his first point.

A fence formed a boundary on the long side of the peninsula, and the land there was short-cropped pasture. The ridges above the creek angled into the fence and formed the long leg of a right triangle whose base was the road. I had marked the sharptails down in about the middle. The best way to hunt this area was to walk the edge of each ridge. There were four of them, like knuckles on a fist.

I expected a wild flush or a bumped bird in the next one hundred yards, but I did not expect a point. A white dog is easy to see, and Butch had the first point of the day with no assist from the veteran, Beans. My part was less perfect. I bounced the bird, leaving a fine cloud of feathers in the air; but it pushed on, set its wings, and collapsed into the tall grass. Both dogs searched the fall area until Butch locked up a second time. I closed the distance between us and on the prairie in front of him saw the sharptail lying low with its head up and eyes watching Butch. It saw me and jumped into the air. Butch leaped after it, knocked it down, and brought it to me.

I was happy and excited, and I praised him to the sky. In return, he made a couple more sweeps as we spent time searching for the others. Since I had ended up at the fence, I was pretty sure the survivors would scatter down the erosion draws to the creek.

"Let's go down the road, boys," I said. "We have all of this day to take the next two, and I want to check out a new place."

The nature of the land in the Missouri Coteau is the opposite of everyone's stereotype of North Dakota. Two years of high water had filled the standard prairie potholes to the status of small lakes. It would have been hard to find a more agreeable landscape. It was a stereotype, not of a barren wasteland, but of pastoral America. If the westward-bound settlers had creaked their way through this land, it would have invited some to stay. And at least one family did, as I discovered at my next stop. Down the road at a Federal Waterfowl Management Unit was a hilltop sod house.

"Boys," I said, as I dug around in the truck's shot drawer, "There are sunflower fields on all sides, a stubble field across a large pothole, and a sod house with a yard full of yellow grass. This place must be the cover girl for prairie birds."

I had to dig out my nontoxic shot—mandated on waterfowl units—and screw the steel-shot tubes into the side-by-side. The ammunition was expensive: ten shells in a box at about a $1.50 a shot. "Therefore," I declared with a resolve I did not feel, "it must be damn good!" I loaded a No. 6 shot Bismuth into the improved-cylinder barrel and a No. 5 shot Estate Tungsten Matrix into the modified.

I immediately walked to the sod house. Bird hunting could wait. I wanted to know who had jumped off the wagon train. A metal sign gave a short history of the home, stating that it was sided at some time in its life but that the siding had been removed to expose the sod walls. A fence had been erected as a token gesture to exclude vandals. I had yet to see my first human being outside of town, so the gesture was probably enough.

I drew the dogs along by voice—the bluestem grass was too thick to see them. The grass thinned out into an old trail that led to a pothole and was lined with plum trees. Beans came out of the bluestem first and made a long cast down the outside of the plum thicket. Butch, long on enthusiasm but short on experience, stayed in the undergrowth. Beans pointed, broke point, then reset into a head-down pose. Two rooster pheasants came up and cackled their way through the plums and across the open prairie. I saw the grass splitting underneath them as they flew: Butch was keeping pace with the birds until he went head over heels.

"Ouch, bet that hurt," I said.

I turned back to Beans and saw that he was out in the grass locked up and facing toward the pothole. Those were most likely sharptails. Pheasants were not rare in this part of North Dakota, but they always lurked in heavy cover.

The sharptails came up early, a seasoned group with some knowledge of hunters. They had a fine laugh and turned out over the water.

"Let's see how good this ammo really is," I said out loud. I swung through and in front of the tail-end bird, then slapped the back trigger. Water geysers burst up around the sharptail, and, like a stricken fighter plane, it splashed into the pothole.

Beans loves to retrieve in water, and wounded sharptails don't dive. He had the bird and was swimming back in the time it took to reload. Butch's first point and retrieve, then a long shot and Bean's water retrieve—how could a day get better?

It couldn't, so it got worse. Butch trotted up. He had hit a bundle of barb wire and was laid open on one side of his chest.

As I have said before, a part of my life was spent in the service of a wartime government, so I don't panic when I see blood. In fact, I had sewed up my setter on several occasions and partners' dogs on several more. Butch's cut was bleeding freely, a dramatic bright red against his white coat. I put him on his back and found no punctures, but I had not brought any of my suturing materials. (Since that day, I have assembled and carried a proper medic's aid kit.) In any case, this looked like a job for a pro. At least I had had the sense to locate the nearest veterinary clinic before arriving yesterday. It was in McClusky, twenty miles away. I gathered my dogs and the sharptail and turned the Ford's nose west to see the doctor.

In small-town North Dakota, you won't find any warm, fuzzy vets specializing in canine plastic surgery. This vet liked bird dogs and understood when I explained the nature of the work that remained in front of Butch for the next few days. "I'll make the stitches strong and tight, and I'll give him a tetanus shot to be sure. Come back in a half hour," said Dr. Kitto.

It was lunch time at Gary's Place. Unlike the Goodrich Machine Co., Gary had a menu. However, very much like the people of Goodrich, his clientele hated to see a stranger dine alone. I was waved over to a table by an old gentleman seated there. "I'm a widower," he explained. "I used to have a hardware store here and grew up just outside of town." We had a fine conversation about local issues that all shared the common threads of "the young folks never come back, and the farming has gone to the big operations." It wasn't just Missouri that had small towns with empty storefronts.

I was late in returning to Dr. Kitto's clinic. Butch was happy. He had a bowl of dog treats and was lying on a rug behind the receptionist's desk. I looked at the vet's seam work. He had used a baseball stitch, and nothing was coming loose. The receptionist advised me to remove the thread in about ten days. "He's such a nice dog, and he's so brave. You be nice to him."

"Yes, Ma'am." I said, unsure that she was going to turn this pampered pet over to me. "I'll make sure he slows down."

"C'mon Butch," I said, then added under my breath, "you sandbagging fraud."

The trip to McClusky had put me closer to the Lone Tree Wildlife Management Area than to Goodrich. Terry Osbourne had marked a location in the northwest side of the area, and, since I was on the west side already, I took the highway north to try it out.

The landmark for my turn after traveling "exactly three miles," according to Terry, was a church. There it was, alone and wind scoured, a solid rock of country Christianity in white clapboard: the Kassel Reformed Church, and two outhouses—all three structures committed to the spiritual and physical well-being of their parishioners. A year or two later I would see these same, unmistakable landmarks pictured in the background of a feature article about expensive, private-lodge goose hunting. The "private" field where the hunters were pitted on Lone Tree was public land. At $400 per day, it made me chuckle. On the other hand, the goose guide, members of the Kassel Reformed Church (and outhouses), and I are the only ones that know about the fraud, and we aren't talking.

The Sheyenne River runs out of water in the northwest corner of the Lone Tree. On the west side, it trickles into the McClusky Canal. On the east side, it becomes Sheyenne Lake, which returns to a river that finds its way to Valley City, then on south of the interstate. My side rises into buttes, earth-sided cuts, and round hills. The agriculture land is on the other side of a valley, but here, where I am, the Sheyenne River is small enough to step across. Generations of men and millions of animals had been through here before me, winding down this valley to the flatland below.

It was the end of the day, and ample memories had been made, but I wanted to take my last bird, and I was willing to put in the miles to do it. At the same time, I didn't want to lose the sense of peace that the view was giving me. I sat with my two best friends on a pile of rocks overlooking mile upon mile of rolling hills, watching ducks and geese flying between them. This was the prairie. Down below was the agricultural land. Pheasants and Hungarian partridge were like those fields—man-made. The sharptail, however, had been here with the buffalo. Not "here" in the broad sense of being in North Dakota, but on this exact spot. It was the same bird, generations removed.

I wanted to turn my luck into gold one more time and take a

sharptail from this very spot to mount as a memory marker. But there were no sunflower fields to shift the odds in my favor, only thickets of chokecherry and buffalo berry. I clicked the gun shut.

"Hunt 'em up, boys!" We had about three hours until dark.

In western parlance, an area like this is called a coulee, a shallow basin with a haphazard source of water that is fed from sidehills and ravines. On the slopes and along the top edge, the thickets of berry bushes hold sharptails when they seek shade in hot weather. But this late afternoon was cool and breezy, so I walked about halfway to the bottom of the leeward side. With a dog on each of my flanks, we covered the rolling ground sometimes a hundred yards apart but still together. Each dog would stop from time to time and look for me. I gave them hand signals indicating the direction I wanted them to go. I stayed under the crest of the hills, like a human contour line, poking in the thickets, then climbing to the next rise. The dogs were free to figure it out; Beans with the experience, and Butch with the pure energy of youth. Experience won out.

Beans pointed a copse of bushes just under the lip of a hill. I was in the bottom, all of four hundred yards away from him. I started to climb as fast as my legs would go, but I was not fast enough. Two grouse flushed up and over his head, cresting the top and going out of sight. Beans broke his point, which was on one side of the cluster of chokecherries, and raced to the top of the hill before spinning around to face the thicket again. The rest of the covey busted out and, apparently seeking the point of least resistance, flew downhill away from him and right over me.

I picked out one bird—the largest of the group—that was flapping and gliding to the left of the others. I never took my eyes from him. I was completely focused on the bird when I raised the double and was still focused when I placed the barrels in front of him and pulled ahead for the shot. I hit him with the center of 1⅛ ounces of copper-plated No. 5 shot and saw exactly where he fell stone dead. This time I did not want a dog to get there first. Fortunately, both shorthairs were looking for the bird on the hillside. They hadn't seen him drop. But I had, right to the inch.

I savored that memory: a perfect male sharptail lying on his belly with both wings spread out just short of a cluster of snowberries. I opened the gun, picked out the shells, and whistled in the dogs. Not only did I have a sharptail suitable for mounting, but the truck was up the hill within a half mile. I had time to make myself the special meal that I had missed when Butch was being sewed up.

Where else but in North Dakota can you break out canvas chairs, feed the dogs, open a beer, and grill the morning's bird for the evening's supper? I had a special marinade of Coca-Cola and soy sauce, and I had even found a jalapeno pepper in a Fargo grocery store on the way to Goodrich. While the grill heated, I cut slices into the breast meat. Then I cut the jalapeno into slivers, discarded the seeds, and inserted the slivers into the marinaded meat. This was a young sharptail, tender and delicious, not an old "blueback" grouse like the one I had shot for mounting.

I wrapped the meat in bacon, placed it on the grill, and set the remainder of my pepper aside. I'd like to think the whole thing brought a tear to my eye, or maybe it was the breeze. Regardless, I lifted my hand, extended the side of my finger, and wiped my eye with the hand that just set down the jalapeno pepper.

A searing, burning, stabbing pain shot through my head. I had to put my hand on the tailgate to keep upright. I howled; my nose ran; my eyes ran; and I ran for the water. I poured cup after cup, as fast as I could fill them, over my face and discovered that water is not an antidote to pepper oil. I wondered if I had blinded myself. No, I thought, Mexico is not filled with citizens clumping around like glass-eyed mice. One thing was for sure: I had gained a new respect for the power of the lowly pepper.

The Sheyenne-coulee sharptail stands on a piece of prairie

wood in my office. It is posed as walking, one foot suspended tentatively in the air as it looks to the side. It is simultaneously the beauty of the prairie, a feathered memory of Butch's first point, Bean's water retrieve, and a reminder to stay away from jalapenos. I look at the bird, between files and appointments with other peoples troubles, and recall the day as often as I wish. A happy memory never wears out.

Chapter Twenty

Messages in the Grass

The shorthairs and I returned to the Sheyenne coulee, passing up the obvious advantages of sunflower edges and stubble fields. My thought was to walk the buttes and cuts until the pickup became a faraway white spot. Somewhere in the bluestem and snowberries, a covey of sharptails was gathered; a small tribe of natives shading themselves from the prairie sun.

I am not, ordinarily, an early riser—ordinary being the schedule I follow while trudging the trials of my livelihood. But on the prairie, I can't seem to stay awake beyond 7:30 P.M., so it's early to bed, early to rise. This morning I was up before sunrise. My new lodging was in a house two blocks from downtown Goodrich. Tim Franz had bought the place to add more rooms to his growing business. It was a white "shoebox," old enough to have been wired after electricity came to town; the wiring ran along the outside of the house entering where convenient. There was no television, no radio, and no telephone, but there were several beds, and breakfast was whatever I wanted to buy and fix. I was happy. On the front of the house a sign said "White." It follows that as the only occupant of the White house, I must also have been elected the chief executive officer. The lack of evidence to the contrary was proof of the fact.

The only upright resident that I could see in my early morning gaze was one of the fifty-gallon drums that occupied the center of every intersection. I suppose there are those who would point with horror at such obstructions to travel and declare them to be road hazards. However, as CEO of the White House, I declared them to be a good and efficient means to collect trash, then I went inside for a bowl of fresh-cooked oatmeal. The dogs were allowed to be inside with me, thus forming my decision-making cabinet.

I had toured the creaky floors between the aisles of the grocery store, breathing the incense of old commerce that you can't find in today's superstores. I bought old-fashioned oatmeal and some more things to cook with my birds. On the window of the creaky door, above the bread sign, was a piece of paper that said, "Reward for the return of my extension ladder, one homemade apple pie." Too bad that I didn't find the extension ladder. I could have used that pie.

My concern about an apparent crime wave (the missing ladder) in the town would not postpone my adventure on the Sheyenne coulee. If I could get going, the sunrise from the survey-marker rock pile would be spectacular.

The sunrise lived up to my expectation, though it was not so much a rising of light as a sinking of darkness. On the prairie, the hilltops brighten first. My rock cairn was on the highest point, and, because I was the tallest point on the prairie, the light of that particular day fell on me first. It brightened the mist of my breath and made the first cloud of the day. I sat and smoked my pipe, letting the sun melt the heavy frost .There was no water or dew—the frost transformed into vapor and was puffed away.

"Let's get 'em boys," I said and slipped the slide forward on the Model 12 Winchester 16 gauge. It was my walking gun, as I have said, and we had miles to go. If I was a bird on this morning, even a shade-loving grouse like the sharptail, I would spend a few minutes stretching my wings in the warming rays. We would work along the sunlit top edges of the buttes. A big wind was predicted for today, and out here a prediction of wind meant something over forty miles per hour. Anything less was considered resting speed.

I cut behind a slant-backed hill intending to scout along the inside edge of two thickets. One cluster was thick and round, higher than its neighbor. A deer path ran between the two. The shadow line of the drop-off was a straight edge drawn across the thicket tops. Beans and Butch were facing me, one behind the other, their attention fixed on the dark shadows under the bushes.

I had heard the Venerables speak of large covey rises, but it was not something I had experienced—until now. Caught between the dogs and my quiet approach, the sharptail covey flushed from dark into light as a "kucking," flapping hooray of feathered confetti. I kept my wits long enough to knock down two. I had a mental impression—a group estimate—of twenty or thirty birds flying across the coulee bottom, up the other side, and on to Bismarck or, perhaps, South Dakota. Sharp-tailed grouse hold a grudge. I would not see them again.

Each dog had a bird to carry, so I led our trio into the sunlight on the front side of the hill, which had been formed into an earthen wall just right for catching rays of early sun. I opened the Winchester and set it against the bank, then eased my back to the dirt and rested my elbows across my knees. A stick caught my eye and I picked it up and poked around with it, knocking loose a clod of dirt from the hillside. A peculiar, cone-shaped lump fell from the clod. I picked it up and rubbed off the dirt. It had a pointed top, was badly gashed, and had several grooves cut around the base. Half of the base was bent in as well, but it was clearly hollow.

"A Minnie ball!" I said out loud. "I found an old bullet. I wonder what it would say if it could talk?" Well, it couldn't, but there was a fellow that could speak on its behalf. A month later, I sent the ball to Steve Schneider, engineer, alchemist, entrepreneur, and black-powder historian.

When Steve is in residence, there are guns, wads, black powder, musket balls, and even bayonets everywhere. Cannon fire is not uncommon. There are clouds of powder smoke, entire fog banks of it. I have thought, from time to time, about the possibility of an errant spark from his fieldstone fireplace landing on an open powder horn. In the aftermath, half of the northern Midwest would be armed by black-powder rifles falling from the air. Steve was just the man to look this bullet over to see what it had to say.

In a month or so he sent me a letter. The bullet was .58 caliber and had been fired from a muzzle-loading Enfield rifle. He knew this by analysis of the rifling marks and the lubricant remaining in the bullet grooves. It corresponded to the type used by the English, and the bullet, by weight, was exactly the right size. Two expeditions had come through this part of North Dakota in the 1840s, basically shooting everything in sight. In those years, Steve told me, there was a lot of game to see, and the appropriate Lord was unlikely to bring ammunition home. The bullet was the probable stray of one or another hunting party. I took his word for it; he had more than a casual acquaintance with lead projectiles.

At the moment of discovery, though, it was just a neat artifact, like an arrowhead or a spear point. I was pleased to have it and buttoned it into my shirt pocket.

The prairie is changeable. I thought we had at least another two or three hours before the wind rose. I was wrong. I could hear it coming from the north in a rush like the noise from an astonished crowd. The sound did not bother me as much as the rolling cloud that I could see racing across the hills. It was a gray color moving across the ground, more an image than a thing. It was just air, but I hunched up when it got to me. One moment it had been quiet, and the next we were in a sustained roar. My peaceful morning blew away with the tumbleweeds. There was no ebb and flow: the wind was a steady river, a current of noise with a persistent push. I walked back to the truck, shoved along like an unwelcome trespasser. It turned out that the prairie wind had something to show me that the grass had forgotten.

I loaded the Ford and drove down the township road into the coulee bottom and across the stream. As I climbed up the other side, a sharptail flushed from the ditch, flared into the wind, and glided to the edge of a windbreak.

"Now, there's an invitation if I ever saw one," I whispered to Beans. He raised his head. Butch had seen the message from start to finish from his spot on the passenger seat. "Why not?" I said. "We came to dance."

I let the dogs out and opened the tailgate. My hat blew inside the camper cover. Crawling on my hands and knees, I picked it up and backed out. Then my gun case and one of my gloves blew back inside the cover. "Well, for heavens sake!" I crawled in a second time. What must it have been like for humans to do even the simplest chore on days like this?

A problem for humans, but no problem for dogs. Both of them were on point out on the grassy flats next to the tree line. The wind was at my back; therefore, I planned the stalk by going to one side of the point, hoping to get a flush into the gale. But, I asked myself, where was the bird?

The answer was, as I quickly learned, with nine others. When they came up, I was on one side, not behind them as I had planned. They were stuck in the wind, tethered like kites. "Piece of cake," I muttered, and picked one out, swung in front, and missed. My target felt the charge go by and swung with the wind, then was gone. No matter. I had two more shots and nine targets. I focused on a second bird and missed again. I stayed on that one, led it some more, and missed a third time. They all looped down the coulee and blew away.

Ten targets, floating like brown-and-white balloons, completely untouched. I was staggered. Could I possibly be that lousy? A mile from here I had shot a double, the first two birds of the morning, and now I blow three shots into the air.

"Into the air!" I hollered. Since the dogs could not fly, as I appeared to be commanding them to do, they hunkered low. My cap blew off a second time. I chased it down and jammed it on my head. "Damn wind!"

Right, I thought. The wind. I was leading birds that were standing still. All I had to do was point right at them. They were going forty miles an hour forward, while the wind was blowing them the same speed backward. "The fundamental principle of the magician's art is misdirection," said Harry Blackstone. He would have been proud of those prairie tricksters.

We needed to move out of the high country. Ducks Unlimited had created the Crystal Lake Wildlife Management Unit east of Goodrich. Maybe the wind would slow down if I moved twenty-five miles. The logic behind that line of thinking makes me giggle now, considering that in North Dakota twenty-five miles is next door. But like the last words of another ill-fated traveler named George Armstrong Custer, "It seemed like a good idea at the time."

The management area was mostly lake, but it had a boundary of prairie up against a sprawling sunflower field. The wind, like

Custer's Indians, had followed my retreat. It also helped me. I could walk the close edge of the sunflowers, putting the crop on my right and the wild land on my left. Sharptails are not often deep in the plantings. They prefer to be near open places. I could cover the edge, and the dogs, with their fine noses, would wind any birds out in the grass. One foot in front of the other, with occasional side-steps to recover my wind-shoved balance, brought me to the end of the field. Beyond it, on all sides, was flattened wheat stubble. "Empty as a sinner's dream," I said to myself.

Empty, that is, except for a single bird beating its wings, then coasting and beating again. On it came, a sharptail with a death wish. I shoot some skeet in the off-season, and even though I know each bird is to be taken over the middle stake, the end position (station 7) has a long incomer from the high house. The temptation to watch this clay is overwhelming because it appears to be getting easier to hit as it gets closer. In fact, it is getting harder to hit because the pattern from the gun gets smaller as the target gets closer. I should have taken my shot when the sharptail was out at twenty-five yards or so. I finally decided to shoot when light sparkled from its eye. I missed, then I missed again. But the third shot, a bonus available in a repeater, found its mark. Both shorthairs came over, and we walked into the sunflowers to pick up the bird.

It was a maze. I thought I had a good mark on the fall, but I found myself walking in circles, unable to make any sense of where I had shot from or where the bird had dropped. It was up to the dogs. I stood in one spot and hoped that they could find the bird and, then, that they could find me. It was impossible to call them. Even the sound of the shot had been snatched away by the wind.

The old man came through. Beans wound his way between the sunflower stalks, carrying the third bird of the day. Now, where was Butch? Time passed, and still no Butch. I blew my whistle, hoping the noise would carry downwind to him. Beans and I walked the crops, weaving our way between the rows, waiting for our scent to bring him in. Instead, I smelled Butch first. Then I saw him, proud as a pimp and smelling twice as nasty. His white coat was now yellowish green. He had found, and probably killed, a North Dakota skunk.

Like father, like son: in a tradition begot by sharptail hunting in Minnesota, Butch had fulfilled his destiny. He was painted, dipped, and sprayed with polecat oil. I had reached my limit of birds, and my day was spread before me. I would not spend it with a book and a nap. It was time to return to the Goodrich Grocery for the ingredients of skunk dip. I hoped they had them.

First, I had to stop at a pay phone. While I knew what to buy, I did not know the recipe's proportions. Right now, fifty gallons did not seem enough. Fortunately, my wife, Cheryl, was home and found the ingredients and directions posted on my downstairs cabinet door.

"Two quarts of hydrogen peroxide," she said, "a bottle of Dawn dish-washing detergent, and a box of baking soda."

"Got it!" I answered. "What are the proportions?"

"Pour both quarts of hydrogen peroxide in a bucket, then add a tablespoon of baking soda and a squirt of the detergent. Oh, and don't mix it up before you need it. It will fizz up. Rub it into the fur, then rinse it off with water. Bye Honey, and good luck."

A nice sentiment, but I could have done without the laughter.

I pulled open the creaky door of the grocery and walked in. Apparently no one had claimed the apple pie or returned the extension ladder because the paper was still posted. That apple pie still sounded good. The owner, a pleasant-looking man with spectacles, was standing behind the cash register. He looked me over— boots, hat, hunting trousers, and whistle lanyard.

"I need two quarts of hydrogen peroxide..." I never finished the order.

"A box of baking soda," the owner interrupted, "and a bottle of

Dawn detergent, along with a plastic bucket and a brush. Yessir, it's all right over there in the corner."

"You've filled this order before," I commented.

"Been a good year for skunks. Don't forget to rinse the dog first. That'll be $8.95."

I drove back to the White House, then found a hose and an outside spigot. Butch was not a good customer for the dog wash. I put the ingredients together and worked them into his fur. I gave thanks to those wise German breeders for a short-haired dog and to whatever chemist had endured the testing phase of the recipe. It worked. Butch was tolerable smelling and bleached as well. He never looked so spanky white.

When I left Goodrich that year, my mind was already making a list of what I would need to make my next stay in the White house more pleasant. At the least, I would need a radio and a desk lamp, and I would bring in one of my camp chairs for a comfortable seat. However, as the wise man said, "Make plans, but don't plan to live them." The following year, my annual call for reservations met the curse of profit.

"Uhmmmm, we have groups of bow hunters now," Tim said. "We're pretty much booked solid through the season."

"Well, I guess I can stay in McClusky, but how about hunting your sunflower fields?"

"Nooooo, the rent was raised, so we save them for the groups."

So long Goodrich. One bird hunter and a couple dogs don't count for much. But I made friends out there, and maybe they wonder whatever happened to that writer guy who liked sharptails. I'll see them all again some day. Lone bird hunters can turn up almost anywhere.

Chapter Twenty-One

Just Right

Ihave a new, orange cap, and I am proud to wear it. I am particular about what I wear on my head and how it looks. I am also superstitious about what it advertises. For instance, I never put a feather in my hunting cap. It's bad luck. It's also a bit too showy. "Hey, look! I killed a bird," isn't a message I want my cap to send. Nor do I want my head to be a billboard for multinational sporting goods corporations. The only label I want my appearance to suggest is competence in bird hunting, which is more of an entire wardrobe message. If a bird doesn't require me to hide, I don't wear camouflage. I don't want a farmer's first impression to label me as an urban guerilla. I also don't want him, or any new acquaintance, to mistake me for a Martha-Stewart-goes-bird-hunting fop or an outdoors-catalog model. No new caps with their bills flat and straight. And forget the neatly pressed "event" shirt tucked into matching, creased hunting trousers. Everything I wear works. When it wears out, I have it repaired.

Today I took my hunting pants to a nice lady to be refaced with new canvas. I finally found a pair of trousers that held together for one year. I wish I could buy a couple more pairs of them, but they are no longer available. The only way I can get something that I like is to have it remade. Two years ago I cut apart some old strap vests and had the nice lady assemble a new one with the features I wanted. It took me twenty years to figure out what a vest ought to be.

What that suggests to me is a problem with the field testers.

Who is using this stuff, anyway? There can't be many bird hunters in China, Sri Lanka, and the Dominican Republic, so I'm afraid I have to lay it at the feet of those most public of hunting models: the video and television personalities. I might as well throw in another offender: the outdoor writer. So, what type of cap, garment, gun, or shells are you using, sir? goes the question.

The answer, to be taken literally, is "Any 'given' brand."

I am proud to wear my new, orange cap to top off my haphazard, personal fashion collection because the cap says in bold letters on its front, "Cenex, Wimbeldon, North Dakota." It was given to me by Dave Carlson, manager, farmer, and hunter of all things furred or feathered. I consider it to be a badge of distinction—like a decoration awarded by a foreign government—for service and valor over miles and miles of prairie walking. Because I owe Dave Carlson, no corporate cap will ever get this one off my head. But for Dave's help, I would have had to start all over again when Goodrich dried up. Stop at the Cenex for gas when you are in town, check the weather scan on his crop computer, and if you pass through in November be sure to walk into the shop and see the deer heads. Some of them have bodies attached, others don't. This is as close to those country-store calendar prints of hunters gathered around the woodstove as we will ever get.

As for the fortunate few who have all of the time in the world to hunt, all of the given brands of gear, and all of the places and occasions to use them, pass on by. Dave is a working man, and one freeloader is enough.

He gave me the grand tour over his noon hour. I had stopped in on my way back east. I consider myself to be an adequate off-road driver, but riding with Dave in his pickup is like taking a lap with Richard Petty on the NASCAR circuit. There's off-road driving, and then there's being with a guy that does it every day. He showed me the country, the prairie trails, gave me permission to hunt the land,

and all but patted me on the head and said, "Go get 'em."

I booked a room in Jamestown and accepted Dave's hospitality. A marathon runner couldn't cover the ground that I worked that first day—my two dogs and I were just too small a boat in an ocean of agriculture and prairie grass. I returned to Dave's in midafternoon for a cup of coffee and some advice on how to shrink the earth into a manageable size. I was finding sharptails, but they were flushing wild. Almost every flock had been in the stubble fields and unapproachable. Only a single had held for a long shot.

"Let's go back out. I'll come with you," he said. "We'll stop at my trailer, get my gun and my dog, then try a smaller spot south of the county road."

You know you have the right guy when his yard has a pile of goose decoys and his gun is a beat-up Remington 870 hanging in the rear window of an old Chevrolet. I pulled into his place and parked out of the way. I had my pipe barely half filled when he walked out and unlatched the dog kennel. Then, both man and dog were in the Chevy pickup—already packed for the purpose—and headed down the road.

We turned off the pavement and onto a dirt two-track, drove over two hills, then bent left, banking into a looping downhill trail. Next, we passed through a coulee bottom and up the side, parking at an old gravel pit. It's the sort of thing that you do out west; ride hard, turn quickly, and haul the horses up short, skidding to a stop. Just another day in the saddle for Dave.

"This is the Seven Mile coulee. From here," he pointed at his feet, "way up to Wimbeldon is a shallow valley. We farm some of it, graze some of it, and some of isn't good for anything, except," and he smiled, "sharptails."

We walked around the gravel piles. There, laid out before me, was a condensed version of my whole day. A prairie coulee on the right, a hillside field of cut alfalfa, and, next to it, a sunflower field.

The last sharptail on earth, if it ever came to that, would be found right here. "This is perfect," I said and sent the dogs on their way.

Halfway down the field, on the hillside, the dogs struck bird scent between the big alfalfa bales. Dave was walking the coulee edge with his retriever. I signaled with a whistle, and he waved me on. Sharptails love fresh-cut alfalfa leaves, and four flushed from the field and "kucked" across our front, trying to make the tall sunflower edge. I had enough time and dropped a bird on the green turf. One of the boys brought it in, but I had no time for petting and smoothing the feathers. Dave, and sunset, wait for no one.

We stopped at the fence. "The land beyond here is a game refuge," Dave said. "We'll hunt the crop edge, then turn back along it toward the gravel pit." I nodded in agreement. Native prairie on the refuge side, crops on our side—a perfect setup.

Dave walked about six rows out into the sunflowers, while I stayed on the fence line. This was a year or two before my quail triple in Oklahoma, so I hadn't seen it done until the sharptails came up in front of Dave's Model 870: five birds went up, and three came down.

"Now, that's shooting!" I exclaimed.

The two survivors, plus seven or eight others, curled out into the crops. They stayed flower-head high until they crested the hill and were gone. I was hoping for stragglers or a new covey on our return trip, but hope doesn't fill the rice bowl. We came up blank and reached the road that we had driven in on.

"Those scatters might have stopped short," Dave said. "Swing out into the stubble, and we'll walk around the plum thicket."

"Short of what? I asked.

"Wimbeldon."

One did stop, and it was a bad mistake. Beans locked into a point at the far edge of the thicket. The bird drove out low and fast, not laughing about it, and died in a fine puff of cream-colored feathers.

"Perfect!" I said. "That's my last of three."

We cleaned our birds in the twilight and buried the entrails in the gravel pit. My new friend declined an invitation for tomorrow.

"I plan to hunt for half a day," I said, "then I'm on the road home. I enjoyed your company, and I thank you. Here," I said, "this is for you; I personalized it. It's a copy of my first book, *Hunting the Sun*, all about the sharptail's cousin. I hope you'll see your way clear to letting me hunt with you next year."

"Count on it," Dave said. "It will get better."

Next year came soon enough. I left home at 7:45 A.M. and was loading my shotgun on Dave's family farm at 12:45 P.M. That included a stop at Clem and Hazel's Corner Cafe for the noon special, desert included. There had been a lot of rain in the last two weeks. The wheat was out of the fields, but the soybeans were still ripening. Sunflower prices were down at planting time, and the commodity brokers must not have been optimistic. The farmers certainly were not. Prairie agriculture had changed from bowing flower heads to the curly oceans of green, yellow, and brown soybean plants. The effect was immediate. There were no sharptails in the usual locations. Eight jumped from the middle of a wheat-stubble field, followed by twenty more. Encouraged by at least the sight of birds, I circled that field, then two more, walking across the adjoining bluestem to any likely looking thicket of willows. Empty-handed and hoping for a repeat of last year's results, the dogs and I returned to the Ford and drove to the bottom of the Seven Mile coulee.

Things had changed there as well. The sunflowers and sharptails of last year had become wheat stubble and Canada geese. Even though North Dakota gives their homeboys a week's advantage on waterfowl hunting, the geese were either migrants from farther north, or they had never been shot at. The dogs and I walked the edge of the field, working the alfalfa planted between the cultivation and the coulee grass. The geese walked along with us, about two hundred yards to our side. Beans is fond of web-footed birds and decided to walk closer. He pointed staunchly. A half-dozen geese walked over to see what he was staring at. He looked at them, and they returned the favor. A North Dakota standoff, each side turning its head in that questioning tilt. Beans quit first. There was work to be done.

We don't make much noise. No bells, no beepers, no hollering, just the shuffle of boots and dog pads eating up the ground between us and the idea of birds rising from thin grass. The wind was in our faces, carrying a promise of more rain and the sight of it in long curtains to the north. I was mulling over different ways to beat slippery mud roads when it happened. A covey came up on our left. They had been feeding on grain scattered in the wheat stubble. We had walked by as the lookouts hunkered the flock down.

What hilarity! A grand joke played on the prairie walkers. Flickering and sailing on creamy-white wings above the gray stubble, they waved good-bye and laughed about it. All of them save one. There is always a straggler, the undecided bargain shopper who rushes out just as the door closes. This one left her skirt on the floor, and the rest of her wardrobe followed when the Winchester 16 gauge cracked.

The rain came on us some distance from the truck. It was not a hard, vindictive storm, just misty company for the rest of the walk. By the time we reached the Ford, the rain had pulled the rest of the day's light down to quitting time. Not a bad afternoon, but the lack of sunflowers and the abundance of soybeans needed some bourbon and a dry bed to think it through. We were wet, tired, and ready for a good rest.

I pulled into the Jamestown Motel. "No Vacancy," the sign read. No problem. I had made my reservations weeks ago.

"We don't seem to have your reservation," said the desk clerk. "Everything has just been a mess. My folks bought the place, and we're new to the business."

I'm standing in cold, wet field clothes, and she's sorry. Well, facts are facts, and they don't change because we don't like them.

"Does any other place in Jamestown take dogs? I don't want to leave them, or anything, out in the truck." She checked and called a second place, right downtown. They had a vacancy.

"Fine, tell them to hold the room," I said, then grumbled out the door.

It was a nice room, standard city-motel fare. The dogs and I walked down the hallway and caused two nice people to reverse directions. Nothing unusual, just the normal reaction of polite society when confronted with muddy clothes, tired dogs, a bad attitude, and guns.

The morning forecast predicted more rain during the day. The look of the early sky agreed. I needed to leave the city and get a good breakfast. I could do both by driving to the Sportsman Bar Cafe & Gas, one of three buildings in downtown Spiritwood, North Dakota. Red brick outside; a big, wooden bar, and a garage-sale assortment of tables and chairs inside.

I collect old cafes. I have a rating system. If it has jigsaw puzzles on the wall, order anything on the menu. If it has country-and-western-singer posters on the wall, order the special—that's what you're going to get anyway. The Sportsman has beer advertisements. It is the Louvre of Budweiser art; the Guggenheim of the Grain Belt. You don't order breakfast here. You just sit down at the bar and take it all in.

"Whaddaya want with yer eggs? Bacon, ham, or sausage?"

The owner is cooking. I don't have to ask; he looks like the guy who ought to be behind the bar of the Sportsman Bar, Cafe & Gas.

"Bacon, and coffee," I reply. I love this place. It's 7:30 A.M., and a guy at the end of the bar has his first beer of the day. A couple minutes later, two more feed caps walk in and take their places at the bar. I nod, they nod. Two more beers on the bar, without a word, followed by the dice cup. My eggs, bacon, and hot coffee are placed in front of me on a paper plate with plastic silverware. The eggs are perfect and the bacon crisp.

"Whaddaya huntin'?" asks the first feed cap.

"Sharptails," I answer.

"Whereabouts?"

"Carlson place."

"Nice folks. He died this year. They had seven kids. You know one of 'em, then?"

"Dave," I reply.

My credentials having been examined, I am now one of the boys.

"Yah, I seen yer hat. Git 'im a beer."

"Thanks," I said, though the last thing I wanted was a Bud Light for breakfast.

I finished my eggs and my breakfast beer, paid the bill, and turned to the door. "Are you coming back for lunch?" The question came from a stout, little teapot of a lady who walked out from the kitchen with the restaurant's books and cash box in hand. "We're having lasagna."

"Count me in," I said.

"See you, then," she replied.

The whole day seemed brighter than the mumbling mood of the sky. I was heading to the top of Seven Mile coulee. Last year I had found a single bird right at the end of the field road and a covey in the prairie grass. This year I didn't know what to expect other than a long walk. The field was two miles on a side and perched above the rounded lumps of an ancient floodplain. In between the wheat stubble and the bottom land was native prairie and, according to Dave, a rumor of Hungarian partridge.

Bird hunting is mostly gossip, otherwise we never would have had the standard story of a tree full of ruffed grouse shot from the bottom up with a .22-caliber pistol. The coulee top doesn't need a story to draw me in. I would go there just to see the dogs running wide-open across the grass-covered erosion draws. All the planting is done close to the road. A muddy ribbon runs down the middle, two ruts of rich, slippery clay leading out to the prairie grass. There were no sunflowers, just beans—an ocean of soybeans. We made it, but if it rained some more, I might not get the truck back to the gravel. I turned around by driving out on to the prairie and parked the truck facing back the way I came. It wouldn't help, but, then, I still swing my arms before jumping a stream and bounce a basketball a few times before shooting a free throw. It firms up in my mind what the result is supposed to be.

After two hours of strong walking, Dave's rumor was laid to rest. If there were sharptails or huns on this plateau, they didn't live within my narrow corridor of influence. We turned back, resolving to cover the long walk in a head-down, Spartan-stoic, take-your-medicine sort of way. Butch is more optimistic than the old dog and I. He kept working the bean-field edge and proved that a positive attitude prevails. He pointed, relocated, then slow-walked into a final point about four rows into the soybeans. Busted, a young sharptail jumped out of the low jungle and flew back toward me. I can't say that it made the long walk worthwhile, but it definitely helped pass the last few minutes. I pocketed the bird, and we walked the few hundred yards to the truck.

A water break, a smoke, and half of a sandwich still hadn't given me the answer to the problem of sharptails in the soybean ocean. I packed up and drove back into the ruts counting on gravity to get me out.

Then a sharptail flew across my windshield, banked right, and landed on the edge of an open hole in the beans. Sometimes the low spots don't grow the crop, and a small, open bowl is created inside the planting. I had a clear mark on where it landed. The dogs were out, I had my vest on, and we were all in hot pursuit. It didn't take them long to find the grouse. It came up, then went down into the beans. Another flushed to the right, and then a third. I let these two go in the hope that they might betray some of their cousins. They did a fine, treacherous job. Both landed in the next open bowl.

"I have the answer, boys!" I told the dogs. Armed with new information, we crossed the few hundred yards to a dry, shallow depression rimmed by soybeans. Both dogs hit brief points, and six more sharptails came up, giving me my last bird of the day. The first thing I intended to do tomorrow was hunt the slough edges, fertilizer burns, and any other empty spot in the crops.

I drove into Wimbeldon, which was in sight from the field, but not from the road. The road was a wall of rain. It was a monsoon-like downpour. The distance between the curb and the door to the Cenex is only about thirty feet, but I had to sit in the truck for twenty minutes waiting for a break in the deluge.

The rain slowed to a steady patter, and I sprinted for the door. I pulled it open and slid on the floor to a stop by the counter. "He's back!" came a holler from the middle office. "I figured you would be up to your hubs in gumbo."

"I got out just in time. The squall line is probably over my field right now. Isn't anyone picking their beans?" I asked.

"No, and not because they like to leave them out. Half the fields are still green, and some brown ones are too wet. You know how it is, one day of rain means two days wait." Dave turned on the crop computer, mousing over to the weather radar. "Here's the rain, it stretches clear back to Devils Lake."

"That pretty much puts the lock on my bird hunting. All the sharptails are in the beans because that's where the food is." I had opened the crop of my first bird of the day, and it had been stuffed full of soybean pods.

"You're not going to let a little mud stop you?" said Dave with a smile.

"No, I am going to let a lot of mud stop me. I may get back here in November after the deer season. I travel over to Regent, in the southwest part of the state, for pheasants. Problem is, sharptails get jumpy late in the season."

Dave nodded. "They do, but we have pheasants here, too. Not a lot, but enough to make a hunt worthwhile. I'll be done with the fieldwork by then, so stop in. It'll be just right."

"Count on it," I said. "I'm going to swing down to the Sportsman; they have lasagna today. Want to go?"

"No, I have to meet with our board this afternoon. No beer breath allowed," Dave replied.

It rained all the way to Spiritwood. By the time I reached the Sportsman Bar Cafe & Gas, I had decided to pack up and go home. First, however, I had a date with a homemade Italian lunch, a couple of cold beers, and maybe a slice of pie. There is nothing low fat and high fiber in the Sportsman. They have a jar full of pickled pig's feet to prove it.

I think I have found a place to hold on to. A small, 1960s-vintage motel backed up to the James River on the old town highway promises me that they won't lose, or move, my reservation. It has chairs outside the room doors and a sunset-facing wall to tip them up against. The Sportsman serves three meals a day, and I am not partial to any particular menu or foreign ambiance. There's not an overpopulation of sharptails, but if it gets too thin the Lone Tree is within a two-hour drive, and I haven't been blanked on the Seven Mile coulee yet. The Goodrich obstacle has become a new opportunity, and, for the record, I haven't seen a hound dog sleeping in a Wimbeldon street.

Chapter Twenty-Two

Hunting Money

The comb of the prairie wind, the day, the sun, the curtain of rain on the bottom of a curly thunderhead—I don't have to buy these things with money. I have to buy the time to see them, and time is not limitless. I am not among the lucky few who have either all of the time there is—often because they have nothing else—or all of the money, so that they can buy the time.

I have come to terms with time and money as mediums of exchange. It's not enough to know the price; not everything is worth what the purchaser will pay. Stuff is stuff. You buy it, it breaks down, you throw it away, and you never miss it. Now, I must know the value of things, and value is measured by the rule of Victor Hugo, who wrote that "As the purse is emptied, the heart is filled."

We buy tickets to a ball game, green fees to play golf, and pit passes for NASCAR. If what we get in return is a chance to watch Michael Jordan from courtside, a round at Pebble Beach, or an opportunity to touch the racing cars and feel them roar, we rejoice. The soul is enriched. The heart is filled. There has been a fair trade of value. Money has bought the time to do what you want to do.

Money is no stranger to bird hunting. For more than one hundred years, there have been plantations in the south whose owners poured immense sums of money into habitat improvement for the single purpose of producing large numbers of birds to shoot. Twenty coveys a day, together with dogs and horses and handlers to find them, don't come cheap. Those hunters who lack the money-half of the equation had better be prepared to kiss some ass, which may not enrich the soul.

Therein lies the sore spot. Private versus public access to that which fills the heart—our game birds.

It ought to be enough to pay taxes and license fees. The price of the ticket for superb hunting ought to be equal to the published fee. The failure of public areas to meet the expectations of public use is the best example of the difference between price and value. And no bird is a better touchstone than the ring-necked pheasant.

The Asian bird was introduced into Minnesota in the early 1900s. The first hunting season, in 1924, lasted four days. The season length was fewer than seventeen days until the 1940s. By then, pheasants had become so abundant that the season was lengthened to about three weeks. What a time that was. My father befriended a barber from Sleepy Eye, and the two of them watched a field of cut and shocked corn. There were so many pheasants, my father reported, that on the day before the season opened the birds could not be counted. The roosters leaped and sparred in such multitude that the entire field seemed to move. When my brother and I became old enough to hunt, the barber was gone, and so were the pheasants. Even though the season hit thirty days in the 1970s and forty-four days in the 1980s, there was nothing left to hunt. Even the private land had been plowed, and all eyes turned to South Dakota.

The ticket price for the pheasant-hunting value of the 1940s remained a mental block. Taxes plus license equaled wild pheasant. "Wild" implied that there was no difference between private and public land, at least until the public part became empty and the private part held all the birds.

"Hunting for pay, that's what it is, and it's a damn shame. Why when I was a boy there were pheasants everywhere! Now just the damn rich have them," was the mantra of barrooms and barbershops. "The state ought to do something!"

The "state" was doing what it could, given the resources available. The problem was that pheasants were so much fun to hunt—especially when hunting was free—that a flock of birds big enough to offer decent shooting didn't last long. The second problem was that the price of private land, the low profit in crops, and the requirements of good habitat could not coexist. As a result, the private land emptied of birds. In Minnesota, three rooster flushes in a day was considered "pretty good."

Mike McIntosh told me that a town in North Dakota had come up with a different plan. They had solved the problem of no pheasants, a slumping farm economy, and a quiet main street all with one idea—cooperation. They gathered the farmers, merchants, bar owners, and lodging people under one flag. They named it the Cannonball Company, after the Cannonball River, and set out to change their farm land into habitat, their homes into bed-and-breakfast hostels, and their farmers into guides. Oh yes, and the house rule at the Cannonball Saloon had to be strictly obeyed. It read "You are welcome here, just don't scare the horses." Pheasants, lodging, hospitality, and a chance to help the small town of Regent, North

Dakota—all for the exchange of money for time and value.

I had written a few articles for *Shooting Sportsman* magazine. The editor had received an offer from the Cannonball Company to "Come and see what we have done, at our expense." It was the brave, new world of pheasant hunting.

I guess all the masthead columnists were busy in other places, having accepted better offers to more exotic locations than Regent, North Dakota, so the editor passed the offer to me. I had never been a guest anywhere. With that as my sole qualification, I pointed the nose of my old Ford to the west across the Missouri River, then southwest to Regent for the opening day of pheasant season.

Getting over the Missouri River meant crossing a bridge, and the best of the three available was via the interstate through Bismarck. Once across the river, I turned off the four-lane highway into Mandan. I have followed that trail, down State Highway 6, ever since. The prairie is best seen from a two-lane blacktop.

There is an old train station—now a museum—in Mandan. Right across the street is a grand hotel—now converted to office space. It is easy to imagine a steam train unloading sportsmen and dogs, guns and gear; all of it hauled across the street in steel-wheeled carts. Steak and cigars for dinner, some cards, and a late night into an early morning sunrise. Then back across the street, and on the train again for a slow and easy pull to the hunting grounds.

Driving with the windows down in early October brings the dust and smell of the prairie into my cab. It isn't hard for a Minnesota forest dweller to see the color of unlimited horizons. It's a light blue in the late-afternoon hill shadows.

I turned left in Mott, then drove downhill to the bridge. There on the highway was a fine rooster pheasant, strutting and bowing. "That has to be the Chamber of Commerce's pet bird," I said to myself. It wasn't. Ten miles up the road, I began seeing pheasants in every field and in every ditch. It stayed that way right into Regent.

The Cannonball Company was located in the back of a wood-sided building on Main Street. A wiry, little fellow was on a step-ladder nailing a company sign on the wall. He was being supervised by a black-and-white springer spaniel.

I got out of the truck and stretched my legs by walking across the gravel street. "The sign says this is the place," I said. He finished the job, got down, and extended his hand.

"I'm Pat Candrian, the manager. This is Rocky, the boss," he said, nodding toward the springer. Both had grins as wide as the horizon. I introduced myself and asked after Mike McIntosh.

"He's over at the saloon with some of the others. You'll both be staying at the Vern and Barb Mayer farm. Barb says supper is at 6 P.M."

"I thought it was just a breakfast sort of deal," I replied.

"It is, but at Barb's it's hard to tell where one meal ends and another begins." Pat laughs a lot. He has a contagious sort of good humor. You know, like a springer spaniel. "Here's some drink chips. I'll come and get you when its time."

Friendly shadows. It's two steps up off the street into the saloon, but I knew the place was a good one. It had a lot of beer posters and a big, long, wooden bar. The ceiling was covered with dollar bills that had been wrapped around thumbtacks and thrown upward. The saloon was filled with happy noise and the butternut and orange of hunting clothes. Mike had found a corner by the card game and some out-of-state acquaintances. Being a good Norwegian, I sat down and listened. It was good to see my old friend once again at home in his prime habitat—the company of bird hunters.

"What this place needs is a pair of swinging doors," I shouted. His hearing is as bad as mine. "Whores would be nice," he answered.

"No, no. Oh forget it," I shrugged and lit my pipe.

Prime rib and browned potatoes, fresh bread and wine, all on a dinner table seated with a West Virginian and his law-school classmate (now in Alaska), an import from Georgia with his son, and several other men. I learned about winter peas from Vern, the farm-owner, who happens to be an engineer by profession. You wouldn't think that a crop of winter peas was much of a dinner-table topic, but it was a fine illustration of the original thinking applied to the problems of agricultural production.

Briefly, peas are planted late and grow until the frost kills them. Because peas are small, the produce is used as bird food for the feeders in metropolitan Williston; thus, it is a profitable crop. How-ever, the vines collapse and can't be picked up with a combine. Vern solved the problem by planting mustard and peas together. The mustard grew first in small but sturdy, upright shapes, and the pea vines tangled themselves around the stalks. The peas freeze, and the mustard plants hold them up for the combine. "Voila," Vern said. "I combine both crops, then separate out the peas from the mustard seeds."

Vern went on to explain that the climate is one of the reasons Regent has such good pheasant production. "The snow comes, it melts off, then it returns. The birds can find forage." He also laid out more of that original thinking. "We plant grain crops and cut the harvest like hay, putting it up in big bales. The bales are hauled down to the wintering areas and provide both food and shelter. At the end of the winter, you can't find a single bale—the pheasants tear them apart to get at the grain."

Each farmer/member of the Cannonball group converted part of their agricultural acreage into big fencerows and grassy water-ways. Some crops were left in the fields as food. Guides kept track of where each pheasant was shot, and at the end of the season the farmers were paid a price for every bird taken on their land. The return from the birds compensated the landowner for the land lost from crop production. The remaining profit was divided up among the company members.

The West Virginian added his endorsement. "This evening we

drove down to the river. I'd say we put up over six hundred pheasants!" I couldn't second the comment, but I saw a flock in a graveyard on my way into town: counting in fives, I got up to seventy before quitting. I thought of my dad's memory, and I no longer considered it to be pumping up the story for the kids.

In the morning, we drove part of the way to the Cannonball River bottom on a dusty two-rut track. Until I looked at the speedometer, I didn't know that a pheasant could run thirty miles an hour. We drove past more pheasants picking gravel at 9 A.M. than I had seen alive in thirty years.

Mike and I, together with Pat Candrian, started the hunt following Beans on a sunny hillside leading down to the river. At that time, he was a young dog with limited ringneck experience. He had handled a few pheasants in my final two years in Missouri, plus a few more as out-of-season surprises during our first sharptail hunts. Beans had a lot of bird scent to sort out, but he found a familiar smell—a sharptail that flushed and climbed into the sky. I had traveled an extra two hundred fifty miles, and the first bird within range turned out to be a prairie native. If it had continued in its first flight plan, it could have gone on to South Dakota, but for reasons known only to its own logic, the bird turned in a long circle and flew back over me. It was, in one opportunity, a splendid chance to have a flashy shot and a better chance to miss in front of an audience. I was carrying my AyA 12-gauge double, loaded with an ounce and one-eighth of No. 5 shot. I shoved the barrels in front of the bird, kept moving, and pressed the back trigger.

It worked. I brought the grouse down on the first shot, and Beans made the retrieve. The first Regent game bird was in the bag, but we had no pheasants yet. Beans and I walked the riverbank, while Mike and Pat paralleled our direction. All of us were kicking up hen pheasants from underfoot and under the dog's nose. The Cannonball River had become a dirt-sided gorge, so Beans and I slid down to the water and continued up the river's edge.

Someone hollered, "Rooster!" I heard one shot and was ready when the ringneck flew across the blue band of sky above the river. I snapped a shot into the space between the rooster's head and the other side of the riverbank. It dropped and hit the water, bobbing along in the current with its tail hoisted like a sail. I needed a Labrador, but only for a moment. Beans had seen the bird fall and was swimming out to get it. A great shot followed by a great retrieve. How much better could it get? Several thousand times better, as I discovered.

There is a low-water ford that allows a splashy crossing to the opposite side of the Cannonball. Then it's a short climb to a small floodplain bordered by a dirt levee along a crop field. In the distance, what appeared to be a big flock of meadowlarks was coming in our direction, apparently flushed by other Cannonball hunters in the adjoining section. The songbirds grew into big birds, then into at least seventy roosters coming right at us. The whole pack settled into the grassy floodplain. All those birds, and every one a legal target. Even better, every one available and waiting for the four of us, and no other hunters within a mile. I looked at my watch. It was 9:30 A.M. Given the number of birds, if I expected to hunt for any part of a day, I had to put together a plan.

I would shoot only pointed roosters, and only those I could kill with a clean shot. Mike and Pat took one side of the floodplain, Beans and I covered the other. With all the scent that was swirling around in the knee-high grass, Beans had a few false starts, and there were a couple of wild flushes. Then he struck a solid mark, reset a couple times, and pinned the bird. The rooster came up, and I held my shot until too close became close but far enough. Pheasant number two fell, and the whole flock lifted up around me. It would have been child's play to shoot the last rooster, but I had a new plan. Mike collected one or two more birds. I wasn't sure because I was looking at a sight that challenged my comprehension.

I looked out across the stubble of Vern's oilseed planting and saw the surface of the field moving. Pheasants were running en masse, some were flying ahead of the others, all were rushing to huddle in a tree-lined ditch that ran out and away from our location. I tried to come up with a number that would picture what I was seeing. It was a herd, a migration. "There must have be two thousand birds," I said aloud and shook my head in disbelief.

My new plan was fourfold: I would shoot my last bird only if it was pointed; was rising and flying from right to left; was a mature, long-tailed rooster; and was a close, clean shot. I hoped to push the time out to at least 10:30 A.M., but I didn't make it.

We puttered around until noon, had a sandwich in town, and looked bored enough that Pat enlisted our help as drivers. A group of six retired army and navy officers, gentlemen every one but somewhat limited in walking power, needed to fill out their dance card. Mike, myself, Pat, Beans, Rocky the springer, and a couple other volunteers started down the grassy middle of two tree-rows. Our patrons were at the far end. It was like driving a stampede. At any point in time I could see fifty to one hundred birds airborne and homing in on the old soldiers like kamikaze planes. I think they fired in self-defense.

The dining room at the Mayer farm could not have held all the imaginary pheasants that fell to guns that evening. It is fortunate that the size of the bird isn't measured like fish. Arms would have collided.

The next morning I was determined to stretch the day past noon. We worked west from the river along the stubble field of yesterday. Beans handled more pheasants in the first three hours than many dogs work in a lifetime. Best of all, we were not part of a group. It was just three men and one dog. The big flocks are wonderful to see, but we never shot into those whirlwinds. Three hunters can't perform the drive-and-stand maneuvers of a dozen. We had plenty of opportunities though, and three shots later I had my birds, each handpicked, pointed, and killed cleanly.

I had carried those mental pictures of my father's generation for so long that I considered them to be tales that were somewhat short of the truth. In two days I had lived my own stories. Even better, it was not going to go away. I had already made my return plans. My kids had to see this. The Cannonball Company had, with some original thinking, decided that the pheasant could be a cash crop and that the whole experience blended with community. What would I pay for the sight of pheasants beyond counting and a clean bed in a home-cooked environment? The value I received from those good people far exceeded anything I could pay in money. If Pat Candrian had appeared in a puff of smoke in front of my desk and said, "I can show you pheasants beyond number—birds exceeding your dreams—a farmhouse to live in, and wonderful meals to eat," I would have accused him of being the devil, and I probably would have sold my soul to take his offer. All the two days cost me was my time. After that, on later trips, I paid money. And I got my value back a thousandfold.

Chapter Twenty-Three

We Remember the Good Parts

Bob White

September, October, November—the three best months of the year. From green to gone, autumn travels through the trees and the bird seasons. Sharptails are the September birds, pointable and steady until October when they go crazy, then November when they are gone like the leaves. Ruffed grouse are the apple cider of October. Impossible to find and sour in September, they are suddenly ripe, sweet, and plentiful in October. So beautiful and so rare, ruffed-grouse-hunting time cannot be wasted pursuing anything else except, perhaps, migrating ducks when the weather is too foul for the woods. Bare November is for deer hunting; gray and red brown, it is that part of the fall worn down to the white bone of the first snow. Finally, like the cherry on top of a banquet desert, a few days of pheasant hunting to give thanks before the day of the same name.

November pheasant hunting is another world. The roosters that are still alive got that way through their innate, scheming ancestry. A really indulgent father would bring his children to Regent in October, when the ringnecks are still dopey and not so trusting. But I am a grouse hunter first, and I must run my passion down to a quiet fire before hunting the Chinese dragon. None of my kids had hunted pheasants—only grouse—so they had no feeling of being deprived or even shortchanged by the challenge of late-season birds. Things like big, gaudy circus wagons jumping out of knee-high grass were only words. The cold and the snow? Just more of Minnesota, pushed west. Game birds flew through trees, ducks through sleet, and pheasants flew on calendars and magazine covers. November makes a school holiday around Thanksgiving, and the thousands of pheasants from last year had, according to Pat Candrian, been prolific and multiplied in kind.

There were three pheasant rookies in the Ford: Tessa, my eldest child and first hunting buddy; Max, my second student; and Butch, progeny of Beans. Butch had completed his first grouse season with honors, exhibiting the caution and intelligence of his father in the hard-muscled, bony framework of an end-of-season shorthair. We turned left in Mott, and true to the Chamber of Commerce cue, a rooster pheasant walked out from the roadside and crossed the river bridge.

"Look everyone, there's your first North Dakota ringneck." I said. In ten miles the birds were passé. They saw so many pheasants, very obvious on the snowy background, that it ceased to be a topic.

I have thought about it, but I cannot recall when or where I shot my first pheasant. I could take you to the very spot where I killed my first ruffed grouse, my first deer, and even my first duck. I think it must be the circumstances. All of my early pheasant hunting, what little of it there was, happened in a group-shooting format. No single, shining moment stands out. I wanted the experience to be different for my rookies. And it was.

We had our seven-course farmhouse breakfast. The dogs had spent the night in a heated machine shed some distance from the house. I came back from their morning feeding with two weather impressions: it was clear, and it was very cold, as in below zero. I knew the sun would warm the day—that is the nature of the weather in Regent—but the first few hours were going to be steel edged. I hoped that enthusiasm and anticipation would cover a lot of discomfort.

Curt Honeyman had drawn our lot for the day. He took us to a deserted farm east of Regent. We stretched ourselves as thinly as we could, walking abreast in rank. The dogs flowed between the walkers before finally striking a half-dozen birds. Tessa's first pheasant came up in front of her, and she drew down for the kill but nothing happened.

"Dad, my gun won't shoot!" she hollered. I walked over. It was frozen. I had brought it inside, not a good idea for a semiautomatic. I abused its metal parts by opening and slamming the breech until the ice crystal that had locked the sear let go. We reloaded and fired three shots in rapid succession.

"Leave it in the truck for the rest of the trip, Tessa. It will have to stay cold in order to work."

I took one rooster on a long straightaway. It flew on and on, then towered and dropped. Neither of the dogs had a line on the bird, but Curt did. He trotted a hundred yards, then a hundred more, following his line to the spot. He stopped, looked around a bit, then reached down and came up with the rooster. I hoped my dogs were watching. Curt would have gotten the blue ribbon in any retriever trial.

We still had not seen the big flocks, just twenty or thirty birds at the most. Pretty tame stuff for Regent. Curt dropped Max and I and the dogs at the head of a draw, and he and Tessa drove to the other end. She would hunker down in the weeds, and we would hunt the ditch toward her. Both sides of the draw were bordered by wheat stubble, with a half mile of yellow prairie grass and frozen stream fifty to one hundred yards wide up the middle. Max and I stepped in, and the dogs surged forward.

The pheasants rose in waves. First in tens, then in hundreds. The savvy roosters took the early bird route and drew the others with them. But not all of the pheasants flew. Three roosters came up in front of Max off points by Butch and Beans. He dropped three with three shots. Not all at once, but one at a time against a background of rolling, flying, retreating hens and roosters. I can't imagine what it was like for Tessa to be waiting and shivering, watching hundreds and hundreds of pheasants come down the draw straight at her, then swing to the right and out of range. I selected two long-tails from the many that the dogs handled, and filled my limit. Butch was a veteran, Max was blooded and proud, but Tessa had yet to fire a shot.

We adjourned for a lunchbreak, while Curt reviewed his maps. After lunch I drove to the headquarters, where Curt told us that we were going to a spot across the road from Pat Candrian's house.

"Tessa," Curt said, once we had arrived at the spot, "you make a little nest in the ditch grass. Your dad, Max, the dogs, and I will come down that flat waterway right at you. The pheasants won't turn off; they want to go into the trees behind you."

"Okay," she said. Tessa is not one to waste a lot of words when there is business to be done.

It took a few miles of roundabout, but we got to the head of the waterway. I could see Tessa's bright-orange cap as a little spot due north of us. In good game-beater fashion, we started toward her. Halfway and still no birds in the air, I was thinking that the pheasants had already left the theater. The crowd must have decided to walk, because Tessa later reported that she could see movement everywhere in front of her. The first rooster made a bid for the trees. She rose up and shot it.

"Hooray!" We cheered.

Excited by seeing her first bird fall, she trotted over to get it and surprised a second rooster, killing it so fast it was barely under way.

"Sit down, sit down!" yelled Curt.

Tessa hustled back to her hidey-hole, carrying both birds and waving them in the air. She missed the next two incoming shots, but in a grand finale she made a fine shot and dropped a rooster on the road behind her. When I got to her, she was grinning and standing with all three birds wrapped in her arms.

"I did it! I got a limit on my first day!" I suppose it was still cold, but I don't remember. All I recall these days is that smile, like a bright-white flock of snow geese, against tan skin. I don't know what Tessa and Max remember, but I'll bet they could take you to that very spot.

The following morning was overcast and not so bitter. Monty Strand was our gatekeeper, and he gave us a spectacular start. We made a small, crescent-shaped drive along a hilltop bending around a small slough, which exploded from empty grass to several hundred pheasants climbing and cackling. A few wise, old roosters had the lead and drew the cloud to our left, away from the kids. I had one good opportunity and dropped a rooster that Beans ran down and retrieved. Monty straightened the line and assured the young hunters that we would work the other side of the road where the group just landed. No one would get there before us. First, however, we had a whole field in front of us. We had no standers to turn, or to take advantage of, our herd of birds. Try as they might, the dogs could not stop the runners, though they pointed, handled, and helped flush over sixty pheasants each before we reached the field's fence line. The last group, as always, came up at the end. Tessa and I focused on the same bird, an albino pheasant. Neither of us shot since we didn't recognize it as a rooster or, really, anything else. "Maybe a pigeon," she said when we finished the drive. Tessa had killed two on the way, and Max was done. He had found his personal rhythm with pheasants; three birds up, three shots, and three birds down.

We returned to the tree rows of last year's walking-drive that pushed birds to the old soldiers. There was no doubt that pheasants were still present. Birds by the tens and twenties were already lifting off to escape our presence at the road. I held out for a solid point from Butch. He had gained a lot of knowledge but was still confused by running birds. My point, flush, and retrieve came about halfway down the first line of trees. Shortly after, a rooster came up in front of Tessa, but she let it pass.

"Is your gun okay?" I called out.

"Fine, fine," she answered and waved back at me.

Another rooster popped out of the trees, then turned in front of her and flew down the row. Still no shot.

"Are you okay?" I called over.

"Fine, fine," she answered and kept walking up the hens.

We reached the end of the windrow. I wanted to ask her about this new gun shyness but decided to let it be. Tessa took the tree side, while Monty, Max, the dogs, and I went into the grass flats between her row and the next one.

A scheming prairie rooster got himself pinned down by Beans. Tessa walked to the point, gun up, gaze focused out on the horizon. The grand, old dragon came up. It was the one she had been waiting for, and in one smooth movement she shot it down almost instantly.

"That's the one I wanted!" she yelled. Beans made the delivery, and we gathered around and admired the cagey Asian. I counted the tailbars.

"Thirty-two! That's a long one, Tessa. A real keeper."

I leashed Beans and gave her the loop. "I'm going to work Butch into the wind and see if he can get some bird experience between here and the trucks." By the time I walked out on the road, Butch had his master's degree. He found, pointed, and held thirty-five individual roosters. I didn't even count the hens.

After supper, the phone rang at our host's farm. Pat Candrian was on the line and said that a group of hunters at the Cannonball Saloon had learned that I was hunting in Regent. They wanted to buy me a drink and meet the guy who had written the story that brought them here.

"Well, that's pretty nice. So, the article had a good result?" I asked.

"Good result? Our reservations doubled. Three of every four groups came after reading that article. It was the best thing yet. C'mon down and let us pay you back," said Pat.

"I'll be right there."

There was a table of nine windburned young men finishing their last night in Regent. They had come from California, Arizona, and Texas on the faith that I had not exaggerated the hunt.

"Well, did I?" I asked.

"Here's how our last flush went," one of the men said. "All of us, every one, got around a slough of cattails. Nine guys, three shells in each gun. Up come the pheasants. Man, they are everywhere!"

"Right, right," interrupted another fellow. "We fired twenty-seven shells."

They all paused, looked at each other, and roared with laughter.

"We got three!"

The following year I came alone and stayed at a new location called the Prairie Vista. For the first two days, I had the whole place to myself, and the dogs had a heated shop for their kennels. We had snow, of course, and some cold, but the hospitality of Lowell and Marlys Prince filled the space. An Englishman and his business companion from San Diego arrived two days later. They also came because of the article, now two years old. I didn't hunt with them, but through a turn of circumstances I met their group the next day.

My guide was an agreeable, young local fellow. Map in hand, we headed east of Regent to a treeless patchwork of crops and bluestem. Two hunters and two dogs don't make a big impact on the landscape, especially one as empty as our location. Not empty of birds—they are always around—but free from anything over six feet tall. Not a tree for miles.

Therefore, Butch found a porcupine. Beans pointed it first, then Butch came boiling in. He honored for a moment, but when Beans took a little juke step, Butch lost it and dove in for the flush. Unfortunately, porcupines don't flush.

I leashed him and turned to the kid. "Come with me. We're going back to the pickup and pin this stupid ass onto the tailgate. Then I am going to pull every quill, slowly, one at a time!"

"Yessir."

I have taped a Leatherman multitool to the left strap of my vest. It's a lot handier than a knife. Surgical forceps don't seem to be able to grip a quill quite as tightly as Leatherman pliers, especially when the quill is soaked with saliva. As far as the old wives' tale of clipping the end off the quill before pulling it, I have my own rule—if you have it in the pliers, yank it.

I picked up Butch and, with some force, slammed him down on the tailgate. He had a muzzle full of quills. They were in his gums and tongue, and a few more were in his shoulders. The kid sat on the dog's rear, and I held the business end.

"Don't move, you son of a bitch."

"Don't worry, sir, I won't," said my loyal assistant.

"No, no, I'm not talking to you; I'm talking to the dog." He didn't intend to, but he got me chuckling, which helped lighten the task.

I worked fast and was brutally direct. Shorthairs are incredibly tough, and Butch, now thoroughly cowed, lay quiet. I got every quill except a short one that I snapped off. We were back in business.

"If you don't mind," the young man asked, "we can drive back down the road and join the Englishman and the group from Georgia. They don't have good dogs like these or, really, any dogs."

"Sounds good to me," I said. We loaded up and drove to a bread-loaf-shaped hillside. The top of the hill was tree-rowed pasture. We sat in my pickup on the road, which had been cut into the butte and allowed me a great view of the incoming pheasant drive taking place in a cattail swamp at the base of the hill.

I could make out my new acquaintances as two oiled-cotton coats at the end of a line of six brown-canvas coveralls. The Englishman did not miss. The second thing I noticed was a constant stream of birds flowing from the swamp to the field. Occasionally one would cross over the truck.

"Perhaps you should load your gun," my assistant said. "A rooster might come in range."

"Yes, I should do that." I drew the AyA sidelock 12 gauge from its case, taking a position in front of the truck. Three roosters rose in front of the Englishman, he killed one—apparently his last because they all were in range—and the other two climbed into the sky and banked toward me. I selected the trailing bird first and knocked him from the air. The lead bird was just in front as I kept the swing going, went in front of him, and pressed the front trigger. The bird's head dropped, and he arced through the air, down and down. I watched, first with pride, then with horror: the rooster was going to smack down on the hood of my white Ford. Three pounds of projectile would put an impressive dent into the smooth metal.

"Oh, oh," I said and moved to try and catch the bird. I was both too late and lucky. It struck the bumper and rang the steel like a flat-toned bell. "Good shot," said the lad. "Good fortune," I answered. "And we could use some after the quill-pig event."

The pocket radio carried by the boy crackled to life. He spoke, listened, then turned to me. "They want to know if you would join them in the field and bring your dogs."

"Of course," I said and drove down to the group.

I have always liked the sound of the South in a man's voice. There were six of them, two brothers and four cousins. They carried a couple Winchester Model 12 pumps and a variety of other working pieces. It's a hackneyed phrase, but they were the very definition of good old boys. I shook hands all around, shared the porcupine tale, and watched them handle their shotguns. All the actions were open, and no guns were leaned against the vehicles. I said I would be glad to join up. I had one bird left to take, they had eight slots still open.

Their guide from the Cannonball Company was certain that the birds they needed could be taken without standers. We lined up on two of the tree rows and marched nine abreast, filling the grass strips in between the trees. Both dogs opened up their throttles, sweeping up and down the line and rooting the pheasants out of the rows. Some were pointed, some were flushed, some went out on their own.

I had not had a group hunt in years. There is a certain contagious excitement about the controlled chaos of walking, shooting, and happy voices. Beans sensed the practical side of the event and made his retrieves to whoever was closest. Butch decided that I had to carry all of his birds. Three pheasants are a load, but five are a lot heavier. I got my last rooster and added it to the bulk.

I felt a tug at my game bag. "Let me carry some of those." It was my loyal assistant.

"Take 'em all, and thank you," I answered.

"No problem."

He had summed it up. The day that had started so poorly ended with no problem. Well, there was just one—a cultural problem.

The Englishman did not want his birds cleaned.

He was going to take them as is—guts and all. It created quite a stir. I watched him pack his duffle, stuffing the dead roosters in with his clothes, and wondered what the baggage inspectors would have to say about that.

Bob White

BobWhite

Chapter Twenty-Four

Room for One

There is plenty of room for random thoughts along North Dakota Highway 21, a two-lane blacktop that runs westward from its partner road, Highway 6. I don't think about my upcoming pheasant hunt until I make the long curve away from the Missouri River. Then I am no longer traveling, I am planning. The interstate is for making miles; the two-lane blacktops are for dreaming about pointing dogs and bird seasons.

I was driving the prairie roads with a window open. It was mid-November and there was no snow, just the yellow grass, dark-shadowed draws, and blue sky. There was going to be a new wrinkle in my late-season hunt this year. The Cannonball Company was hosting a large group of over twenty hunters. That many men absorb a lot of attention and spend a lot of money. I did some thinking about my past history with groups and the impact they have had on my bird hunting. I was going to feel sad if I had to let go of Regent.

Thoughts drift in, then blow out the window. The prairie vistas west of Flasher were fabulous in the late-afternoon light. Judging from the mandatory rooster at the bridge in Mott and several hundred of his companions along the highway, the bird population had not diminished. There ought to be enough for everybody, as long as I did not get attached to the crowd.

I checked in with Pat Candrian at the Cannonball office in Regent. We had not settled on my accommodations. The big group was at the Prairie Vista. This year, my room was at the Crocus Inn, just three blocks away.

The Crocus Inn was a fine house built originally by a prosperous merchant in Mott. The current owners, Don and Bonnie Gion, bought it and had it hauled to Regent where it was set up in the corner of a city lot. They renovated the inside, restoring the turn-of-the-century charm to everything by using antique furnishings, and added some modern conveniences like televisions and hot showers in every room. They did not have a separate shop or kennel for my dogs, but Bonnie let me set up their portable crates in the sunporch that had a space heater. Good-bye and good night. I was the Lord of the manor with a whole mansion for my pleasure. Not quite the same as the White house in Goodrich, and thank God for it. My room had a four-poster bed, an armoire for my field clothes, and table doilies to remind me to mind my manners. And one other thing: Bonnie kept a battery-powered candle in every window "just so you know there's a light on for you."

If you are the only guest, you get to eat in the kitchen, just like at home. I made my bed and checked the weather. There was no snow, and a balmy sixty degrees borne on a northwest breeze was predicted for the day.

I got up, selected the clothes I would need for the day, and walked into the kitchen to renew my acquaintance with Bonnie. She and I had met a couple years earlier. Don would be along, shortly. They operate the bed-and-breakfast as a pair, sharing the chores. In his real life Don is a farmer outside Regent.

"The Prairie Vista is going to be auctioned in February," she said, after we had established that all persons on both sides of each family were alive, well, employed, and taking nourishment.

"What will Lowell and Marlys do?" I asked.

"Travel and visit their kids."

"What about the bed-and-breakfast?"

"That remains to be seen, Bonnie said. "Their land is up for sale, too."

Lowell and Marlys Prince were the owners of the tree-row parcel where Tessa had killed her big rooster. In addition, I had run Butch through his paces on over thirty roosters, and many more hens, in our half-mile walk back to the trucks. He had cast away his rookie year in one session. The Prince's land was also where Mike McIntosh and I had joined the pheasant drive to the retired generals.

"I'll miss that place, and so will the Cannonball Company. The birds and the land are perfect for your big groups." I was saddened by the news. No Cannonball Saloon, and no Prairie Vista. The business climate around Regent was getting as changeable as the weather.

"There's a new restaurant outside of Mott, maybe you saw it on the way in. It's called the Final Go Around." Bonnie was trying to put a positive spin on the loss. I must have clouded over for a moment, but I regained my light side and commented on the good weather, the number of birds I saw driving in, and my joy at being back in town.

"The Cannonball is thinking about building a lodge," she said.

"I think that would be a mistake," I answered. "Canned hunting is what everyone else offers. I feel like part of the town when I come here. A lodge would put the hunters in one place and the town in another. I can't speak for every guy, but I don't like to be segregated."

Don arrived, and the topic turned to the usual things that all small-town dwellers have in common: pickup trucks, tractors, crops, and, of course, the weather. I loaded the dogs in the truck and drove to the office. No one was around except Pat and Curt Honeyman. Curt is the coach of a girl's basketball team, and my daughter Molly plays on our school's team. The three of us shared a few stories, then Curt and I left early. The big group would be coming in on our heels, so we lost no time getting underway.

Curt knew my inclinations and my dogs—we had hunted together when I brought my kids. Our first walk would be along a creek winding through the hills south and west of Regent. It was a new spot for me.

"We aren't going to put up hundreds of birds in here," he said. "This drain is just wide enough for one man and a couple of dogs. You should be able to kill three roosters even with that 16 gauge." A wide grin followed, which was good because Curt is a tall man with dark eyebrows and a quiet nature. He had that patient "coach tolerance," but I think his players and hunters know when he is "disappointed."

The first cast was short, paralleling the road. Butch pinned four hens and a rooster against the fence, forcing the rooster up. I hit him hard enough, but he coasted across the road, then bounced on the adjoining pasture, scrambled to his feet, and began to trot away.

"Hit him again!" Curt yelled.

There was no need. Butch had watched the bird drop and tackled it. Bird and shorthair rolled into a bundle with Butch coming out on top. He brought the rooster across the road, hopped the ditch, and delivered it, disgruntled and kicking, to my hand.

I missed some shots, the worst display being an incoming "gimme-shot" that left us all groaning. Sorry coach. The best was the last. Both dogs worked the edge of a Conservation Reserve Program field, pointing, releasing for a brief run, and repointing until they caught up to the fugitive, one on each side of him. He broke for open sky and bent back toward me, cursing my dogs and my shooting ability in a Chinese cackle until the load of No. 5 shot snipped his lucky streak.

My afternoon was open. I had studied the maps and found the Indian Creek Wildlife Management Area south and west of Regent. Hungarian partridge and sharp-tailed grouse are found in those parts, though not as plentifully as in other places. A trip out there would also give me a chance to contrast and compare the public land to the Cannonball land.

It was a beautiful setting. The state had created a series of picnic grounds around a small lake. These, in turn, were backed up by native prairie grass and tree lines. All around the management area were fields of grain stubble. I switched off my pheasant-hunting eye and looked over the land as a sharptail hunter. The keys were light grass, hilltops, fence corners, and anything different but not dense. Indian Creek had those features. Unfortunately, the assets had no customers. Pheasants were there—nervous, skittering, wild-flushing birds—but no sharptails or huns. Nevertheless, I had a fine walk on a warm afternoon.

I have this soundtrack that runs in my mind; you know, background music. When I am really content and in the best places, it comes forward and plays a mix of tunes. I never can remember the whole of any song, so they come out in bits and pieces. Everything I remember seems to happen to music. When it strikes me as a good idea, and no one is watching, I dance a little, too. Dancing on the prairie is no problem at Indian Creek. Not only is no one watching, there is no one at all.

I returned to my mansion, fed the dogs, poured myself a mood-enhancing adult beverage, and opened my cooler.

"Tonight I will dine on beef stew, lovingly prepared and stored in this can," I told myself. I found an electric can opener but could not figure out how to do anything except plug it in. I still have a G.I. can opener—a P-38— in my pocket, a gift from a grateful government. This small, metal device folds flat, carries easily, and staves off starvation. If you keep a thing around for thirty-five years, you occasionally find a use for it. The P-38 handled the can easily, and the beef stew warmed just fine in the microwave. Within minutes, I was sitting on the porch full, contented, with a little buzz on. Dark came early, and so did the next morning.

A Bird in the Hand

I don't need an alarm when I am on hunting time. If a fellow dumps all of his daily cares and tells himself what time he wants to get up, it just happens. Predictions were for another sunny day with the temperature around fifty-six degrees and a northwest breeze rising into a stiff afternoon wind. Last year it was subzero with knee-deep snow; this year it's shirtsleeve weather. I had breakfast with Bonnie, then I was out the door and two blocks over to the office.

"We're going to the Cannonball draws this morning," said Curt.

"Great!" I said. "And no snow." Better yet, there is a bluff overlooking the river. According to local lore, it was a buffalo jump where the Indians drove bison off the cliff to crash onto the rocks below. Just the historical ambiance I like; slaughter in the midst of plenty.

We reined in the pickups, chasing twenty or thirty birds out of the stubble. I watched the roosters land in the chokecherry bushes that spread out along the fringe of the nearest ravine.

"Looks like the residents are in," I said. Curt stood quietly, hands in his pockets. No sales pitch is required when the product shelves are full.

Pheasants are not buffalo. They have wings, and, in spite of restaurant ads to the contrary, buffalo do not. November roosters know that trucks do not bring good news and that bird dogs are not simply curious. Bird dogs are predators, and pheasants are the prey.

We walked, pausing to kick up hens that the dogs had pointed. We walked some more, and in the process I killed two roosters. But those are not the ones I remember. There are three roosters, still flying, that I will never forget. I needed only one more bird for a limit when Butch made a fine point on a nearby ridgetop. I got too close for comfort, and the ringneck flushed, black against the sky. The Model 12 came up, I swung past the white neck-ring, doubled the lead, and down it came into the tall grass with what I imagined to be a thud, a perfect example of a clean kill. I slipped the action open and caught the empty. All done, at 9:30 A.M. Butch ran over for the retrieve.

Not so fast, said John Ringneck. He leaped up into the air, cackling, and flew off.

"I haven't seen that before!" said Curt, a veteran of countless kills.

"How much deader can a bird get?" I wondered aloud. We climbed the hill. It was open stubble field all around. Not a dark lump in sight, and we could see for a couple miles. The dogs and hunters searched all available hidey holes, but no rooster.

We pressed on another one hundred yards. This time Beans flushed a rooster from my right. It crossed well within range, and when the sight picture looked right, I slapped the trigger. The bird threw his head back and fell, wings clamped to his side, into the ravine. This time the "thud" was not mental, it was audible. I heard him hit the ground.

Well, that makes up for the first blunder, I thought, and watched Beans run in for the pick up. Up came the rooster, loud and proud. The heathen bird laughed at me and my next two shots, flying down the ravine until he was a small, black spot.

"That's twice," said Curt, "I think you need to shorten up your lead. You're stunning 'em."

"Yeah, catch and release, a new conservation method," I answered. But I was shaken. The Model 12 had been the death adder for all pheasants—one shot for each bird—up to this moment.

As a prelude to the next, and last, rooster of the morning, I will tell you that I had not chambered a new shell. The last bird had taken three shots. I seldom, if ever, shoot three times, so following old habits, I slipped two loads into the magazine.

Time and distance passed. We approached an old, wooden trestle, and both dogs pointed a clump of grass at the bottom. Curt came up the draw as I walked across the top and slid to the bottom. It was so perfect that magazine writers would have been clicking pictures. At this moment, I can see the rooster flushing, his back to me as he climbed straight up the ditch bank. I swung from the bottom, crossed his head, and pressed the trigger.

The only sound I heard was a mild "Click." And the rooster was gone.

I hazarded a look at Curt. His face said that I had dropped the ball on an easy layup, then kicked it into the stands.

A day's last pheasant can prove to be a problem. We walked the draws, climbed the buffalo jump, forded the river, and came out on a plain stretching back to the trucks. It was my last chance for a limit. No problem. The dogs had found gold. But it turned out to be feathered fool's gold—a flock of hens. Curt and I and two dogs moved at least three hundred of them, and not a rooster in the pack.

After lunch, Curt told me that he had scheduled a practice with his team, anticipating my early finish. "I saw a big flock across the highway from the tree rows."

"Yeah, I know where that is," I replied and assured him that I would get along fine. In fact, I looked forward to having that slice of pheasant heaven all to myself. The cover was a long, tree-filled ditch that ran from the road to a hardwood grove in the middle of two agricultural fields. From there it stretched a mile or so and was almost entirely covered with prairie grass and cattails. Since I had no blockers, my best hope would be to slip in quietly and hope for some early flushes. After that, I would have to push the birds aggressively or they would leave me behind in a mass rush to cross the highway into the adjacent tree rows.

Neither plan worked. I had pheasants everywhere doing everything. Some flew behind, most went ahead, a lot went to the sides. I had traded my 16-gauge Model 12 for the AyA side-by-side 12 gauge, thinking that I would need the extra power. I outsmarted myself.

The first chaos became a mass rush to the hardwood grove. A lot of the birds must have flown right on through the trees, but some stayed because both of my dogs were locked up on a widespread point. I hustled across the stubble and came up between them, stepping into the grass edge. I expected a multiple rise but not a wall of wings. The closest bird to me was a fine rooster. I covered his head and pressed the trigger. He fell, and so did one more flying behind it.

"Oh, oh." Each dog picked up a prize and delivered the two birds. I had one too many roosters. My first two birds of the day were back at the cleaning shack, and I still had two days to hunt, so my problem was technical. If I left the rooster in the ditch, it would be wanton waste. If I kept it, I would exceed my daily limit.

"I'm sure not going to leave it," I told the dogs. "Mark me down as a game hog, a happy one, and accidentally piggish. I have a pure heart, but I'm too lucky for my own good. I throw myself on the mercy of the court."

The new restaurant in Mott was not open. I had the nightly special at another cafe and a cold beer while watching the completion of the cribbage tournament. Then, a quiet drive home into the long, orange line of the day's end.

I guess two days of sun is the prairie limit. A hard freeze had stiffened the morning into gray November. Curt had a day off, and the Cannonball was full to the brim with orange vests and heavy clothes. I counted nine vehicles and six dogs of varying description. The army had arrived early, buoyed by the previous day's good results and keen on a repeat. I had a new guide: Brad Pauley, a tall, lanky westerner from the Scranton neighborhood to the south. I had shared after-hunt beers with Brad yesterday, sitting at the office table with the guides. He and I would hunt a small cattail slough where two dogs and two men could do some good.

We put up a bunch of pheasants, but they were all hens. Changing the hunt to the other side of the highway, we worked an eighty-acre square of Conservation Reserve Program land. There were roosters in the flock we rousted, and one of them carried a load of

No. 5 shot to the far edge before falling onto an earthen dike. Brad split off with his little Labrador retriever, Morgan, while the pointing dogs and I finished the walk. The roosters in that field stayed away from me, choosing, instead, to fly early and far.

"Let's go three miles over to the front end of this drain," Brad said, pointing to a big butte prominent in the east. "We can enter that valley and come this way. The birds should be down in the heavy grass staying warm."

It was a good plan. We had penetrated only the first two hundred yards of swamp when the slough grass erupted in roosters. Killing two out of the mass of several hundred was done in quick time.

"I'm thinking that all the pheasants are still in here," Brad said. "We didn't stir them up too bad. Let's drive over to the fields where the big group is at and tell them what we saw here."

"I'd like to do that," I replied. I had never been a spectator at a full-dress pheasant drive. Brad had told me that there were twenty-seven guns in the group, along with three guides. My dance card was punched, and if they put up some huns I could spin off and hunt them. "Let's go!"

We drove up and parked with the vehicles belonging to the blockers. Nine men stood waiting for a long line of orange walkers coming toward us. I sat in the truck and took it all in. Occasionally, birds would rise and bank to one side or the other; others would try to fly back across the line. At least two-thirds were hens, and dogs were bouncing and moving in all directions. Three or four men gathered in one spot, stood for awhile, then one of them bent down and picked up his dog. He carried it out of the field and to the back of an open truck. Curious, I walked over. The wind had picked up, and shards of corn leaves blew across the plowed furrows. The previous warmth was gone. A couple of hunters stood at the tailgate, and the dog—a small German shorthair—was trying to stand up. I asked the fellow holding it what had happened.

"Don't know," he answered, "she just went down and couldn't stand up again."

"Why is she all wet?" I asked.

"We poured water on her," he replied. "We thought it might be heat exhaustion."

"It's forty degrees out here, with a wind. Let me look at her gums." I had seen this condition before, and once I gave mouth-to-mouth resuscitation to a partner's dog that had collapsed in the heat. The shorthair's gums were pink, and her eyes were clear. She shivered uncontrollably. "Just a minute, I'll be back."

I trotted to my truck and got a dry towel. I figured the dog had not hunted much, was out of shape, and had run herself into exhaustion in all of the excitement. A couple years before, I had won a prize at a field trial; an energy-boosting powder that mixed with water. One of the trial winners, seeing the bucket in my hand, told me that it was a great product.

"You can have a dog burned down," he said, "and give him a bowl of water mixed with this stuff, and in half an hour he is ready to go back at it." I had used it ever since with just those results.

I mixed up a bowl and took it back with me. She drank the whole bowl while I toweled her off. There was plenty of time as the army milled around, so I got her a second bowlful. She drank that, too.

"Give her some rest. She'll be fine."

Brad convinced the group guides to hunt where we had been. The roosters must have been listening, because when the hunters climbed the side of the big butte only about a half-dozen birds were taken. Plans were made, schemes were hatched, and all left in a cloud of dust for another, larger venue. I decided to go home and put my feet up. About halfway to Regent, I turned around. There was simply no better entertainment, anywhere. I had to see how this operation turned out.

The little female shorthair had made a complete recovery. From my vantage point on a township road, I could see the orange line, surging in one spot and lagging in another, as it approached the standers. This time the roosters were cooperating. Leading all dogs, the little shorthair popped onto the road. The stander closest to me was a pretty fair shot, and as he connected with the pheasants, he would trot over and pick up his kill, then trot back and drop it in a pile on the road. The shorthair jumped back into the ditch weeds and disappeared. Her man flushed and killed a rooster, dropping the bird into the opposite field. He ran across the road and started digging around in the grass for his prize. He must have called the dog, because she came out on the road a second time. She looked over at him, then down at the stander's pile of pheasants.

"Here's one!" she thought and scooped it up, bringing it to her owner.

I couldn't hear it, but the scene played out like a silent movie. "Good dog, good dog." Both owner and canine are happy. So happy, in fact, that she returned to the pile and brought him another one. "Well! I must have gotten two!"

Meantime, the capable stander has connected again, picked up his rooster, and returned to find his cache of birds reduced by two-thirds. You can't buy a ticket to that kind of comedy.

My last day was sunny and crisp, with a predicted high of thirty-two degrees. Even better, Brad had lined up a frozen creek bottom, part of the Indian Creek system east of the management area. It was perfect, custom made for one man and two dogs. Brad would drive to the far end and wait for me. I had two miles of grassy ravine bordered on both sides by grain stubble. And it was all mine from start to finish. I took the first rooster right off the end of Butch's nose and dumped it in the stubble field. A second followed the first within fifty yards. This was going to be a cakewalk.

However, as I said, final birds are often problematic. I hit a rooster, skidded it across the ice, and piled it into a swamp-grass edge, but couldn't find it. A half-mile farther, the dogs made a double point, one behind the other, both facing downhill. It was so pretty that I took a picture, put the camera away, picked up the 16 gauge, and flushed the bird off the bank. It flew across the stream, giving me a shot down on it. I not only whacked it out of the air, I was able to mark the very weed that it struck when it piled up. I couldn't find that one either. By the time I met Brad, I was in a state of despair. Although we returned with his Labrador retriever and stomped the creek bank flat, I was still one bird short.

Undaunted, Brad headed for the Cannonball River. The company had some food plots, he explained, and while the roosters would be a problem to corral, they were in the plots. He was right on both counts. But love conquered my last rooster. A group of four hens flew from the end of my food patch, drawing two ring-necks with them. They cleared the hill and disappeared. I hadn't shot, therefore I hoped they would settle on the lee side. The day's hunt ended right there in the ankle-high grass of that prairie hill. My dogs came over the crest, turned into the wind, and locked down on birds just under the hilltop. I came up from below them, trapping the pheasants between us. The five birds came up as one, four flew on, and I walked over the hill carrying my last rooster.

Brad was smiling, "Well, Ted, I heard you shoot over there, and I said a little prayer."

"With all that help I couldn't miss," I replied.

I had dinner that night at the Final Go Around in Mott. I came early and without reservations. "No problem," the hostess said. "You're just one guy, we'll find room." I had a superb steak, and, better yet, the three young women who were clearing tables came over and talked to me, because, they said, "It's not good to eat alone."

Maybe, but if I had had company, or, for that matter, twenty-seven other guys with me, I doubt if any of those good things would have happened.

Bob White

Chapter Twenty-Five

A Place in the Choir

"All God's chill'in got a place in the choir," the song goes, "some sing low, and some sing higher." That's the way it is with preserve hunting. It's not wild-bird hunting and was never meant to be. It's a playing field, and the ball is a bird. The goal is to imitate the ideal, not to attain it, because the cover and the quarry are not real. You don't have to be an expert hunter to criticize the experience. I confess that I was once conflicted with preserve hunting. The birds are sprinkled out, dogs find them, then they flush and die. Some are shot and some aren't, but they all die. The whole experience seemed to fly in the face of fair chase—the bird ought to have a chance to get away. Then, after one bad experience and several good ones, I came to see it as a game entirely separate from hunting and more like clay-bird games.

There are three primary preserve birds: pheasants, bobwhites, and chukars, all pen raised. That's the thing that distinguishes preserve hunting. Pen-raised birds aren't better or worse than wild birds, they're simply different. Sometimes a guy plays tournament-level golf, and sometimes he plays miniature golf. It's all fun. In my book, shooting is enjoyable any time and any place.

Well, once it was not so fun. My first preserve shoot came by way of a generous invitation from a great fellow with whom I enjoy spending time. The reason I went was to share good company. It was a no pressure "shoot," not a hunt. But on this day the pressure was not only low, it wasn't there at all. The ground was covered with knee-deep snow, and the bird boy had used an all-terrain vehicle to haul pheasants out to the planting locations. A little challenge would have been nice—following vehicle tracks and footprints directly to hapless pheasants buried in the snow was anything but challenging. Too cold to fly and too stiff to keep away from the dogs, every bird was retrieved to hand. My friend and I took turns tossing them into the air, trying to get them out and away to avoid a mess.

In any sport played well, execution is everything. I didn't experience that until a year later when the prospect of good company was, once again, too appealing.

Steve Schneider had traveled from his Milwaukee home. His companions, as usual, were two black-powder guns: a single-barreled flintlock 12 gauge, and a double-barreled flintlock 20 gauge. He brought with him Ben Moore, another Milwaukee native, who was not only good company but was the guy that carried my version of the holy grail, a Boss 20-gauge sidelock double. Now, with Ben's permission, I could shoot it and, hopefully, kill a pheasant with it. I could have cared less whether the creature was accommodating or crazed—Excaliber was in my hands!

The place where we gathered to shoot beautiful guns was a hunting preserve attached by a tenuous road to the Boy River. It was not the end of the world, but you could see it from there. "Wild" by location and by design, Bader's Pheasant Run was a different environment than where I had been the first time. Yes, the birds were pen raised and the dogs could find them, but not quite so easily and certainly not as quickly. I killed a pheasant with the Boss side-by-side and got a chukar to boot. Then Steve handed me the flintlock double-barreled 20 gauge. "Shoot twice, always," he cautioned. "I don't want to be loading an empty barrel attached to a loaded one."

"Okay, twice. I can do that," I answered. However, he forgot to tell me the second most important thing—when the dog is on point and you approach the flush, you have to remember to cock the hammers. I didn't. It was very humbling but great fun.

A preserve is an accommodating place with polite birds. If you screw up once, it doesn't matter and won't ruin your chances for the balance of the day. It is bird hunting without the guesswork. Clients know ahead of time where to hunt, that the birds are there, how many have been put out, and that they'll be close enough for a shot. The greatest challenge a well-run operation can offer is to enhance the one thing you don't know exactly: where the birds are. That's where dogs come in.

My shorthairs know the difference between wild and pen-raised birds. I suspect preserve pheasants have some trace of human scent on them, some small clue that allows a seasoned dog to take a vacation from real work. My dogs point pen-raised birds nose to the beak. These are the same dogs that won't crowd a ruffed grouse and charge ahead of wild-running roosters in order to double back and cut them off. None of that happens on preserve grounds. They play them like pop flies and slow grounders.

My friend George Vukobratovich lives in Florida. With a name like that you know he spent his formative years on the streets of Chicago. George was on vacation with his brothers, Dan and Bob, some nephews, and company employees. Gathered together and armed, like they were this year, they resembled gangsters in canvas coats. I'm not saying that they are intimidating or ugly. Quite the contrary; you couldn't find better manners in church. You just wouldn't want them to go with you to a farmer's door when you asked permission to hunt. The farmer would probably wonder whether the bank had adopted new methods of debt collection. George thought it would be fun to spend their last few Minnesota-lake-vacation days shooting pheasants. George's homebase is on Leech Lake, so Bader's Pheasant Run was the playing field of choice.

He invited me to come along. Actually, he invited the dogs, and I provided their transportation. George and I go back a ways, and

Bader's had become an annual event. He wanted his brothers to hunt over pointing dogs, so he had fifteen birds put out for the morning shoot and twenty for the afternoon. I had a short talk about walking in on a point and the importance of shooting into the blue, never toward the ground, and avoiding low shots.

"These birds will not fly far. Chances are that a low bird will land after a short flight, so remember the motto: If it's low, let it go. All agreed, and we were off.

Butch made quick work of the first twenty yards, locked down tight, and from his demeanor was one step short of chomping the first find. Everyone stopped.

"Walk in from the side, so Butch can see you, and keep your eyes ahead of the dog," I said. One of the brothers, Dan or Bob, came forward stepping like he was afraid of tripping a mine. He got to the dog and did the natural thing. He stopped.

He looked over at me. "No bird," said his eyes.

Well, you know what happened; his pause triggered the flush from right under his feet. The pheasant grabbed for the sky, and at the gun's roar, the bird's head continued forward while the rest fell in a heap.

I carried the body over and stuffed it in his game bag. "You might want to let them get out a bit farther."

"Man, was that great or what!" he said. And so it went.

After the first ten birds, my gang of wiseguys just followed the dogs, taking turns and cheering every flush. We killed seventeen—all of the planted birds, plus two more—and returned to the clubhouse for a sit-down dinner of baked pheasant. It was paper plates and plastic ware, but the food was great, and we replayed every shot. Their gun handling had been safe, and everyone had been successful. The first half of the day was a winner.

The afternoon warmed up a bit too much. Between poor scenting conditions, and missed birds, we collected seventeen of the twenty. We ended the day with cold beer, while the birds were being cleaned and packaged. Everyone had a bag of game, a lot of walking, the chance to shoot at flying birds, and new stories to tell. We could have watched a ball game or played golf. Instead, we looked for hidden birds, found them, and shot them.

This is a popular pastime. Deb Bader, preserve owner and cook, told me that they go through several thousand pheasants a season. I saw it myself. On George's second day, the field had to be reserved because each of the areas was booked. At noon, the clubhouse was filled with men and a few women and kids, all there to spend their afternoon chasing "tame" birds.

The reason that preserve hunting has this appeal is that it takes the body-count factor out of a luck-based pastime. Americans love a guaranteed return. If the popularity of hunting has waned over the years, it is because game and the land on which to hunt it have become scarce. "There's nothing or nowhere to hunt!" say the complaints. Or "it's too cold or too hot or too windy." Preserve hunting lets a person pick his day, his weather, his bird, and his way through a flat, grassy field. Just like porridge—not too hot and not too cold, but just right. You pay your money, you got the birds. Whether you kill them or not is your problem. A preserve operator has to be sure that the challenge is present but not overwhelming. It's not a vision quest.

So, I decided to lighten up and accept preserve hunting for what it is; a walk with friends on a nice day, guaranteed to be interrupted on occasion by a dog finding a reason to come out in the first place. When the bird comes up, the people shoot it. The bird is not seeking its freedom. It isn't mated for life. It's not Bambi or Dumbo. Its function on earth is to be shot and eaten. The difference between a bird in the air and one in the market is that you have to shoot one of them. It's going to die either way. They weren't raised by the thousands to repopulate the prairie.

Look at it as a clay bird you can eat.

Chapter Twenty-Six

Is and Was

The fine mingling of holding on and letting go. As I said at the beginning, I have held on to and I have let go of places, people, dogs, guns, and game birds all in pursuit of six hours of life without a care in the world. Is it worth it?

Because bird season lasts only three of twelve months, I try to spend the balance of my free hours doing something besides drinking bourbon and reflecting on past memories. I accomplish this by preparing for the next season. I shoot clays whenever I get the chance, run my dogs in local field trials, and study the land for more places to hunt.

We bird hunters have competition. A good grouse cover has a wonderful variety of vegetation, of shrubs and berries and trees, and, because it is a thriving environment, numerous small birds and mammals are pleased to make it their home. Emotionally worn urban dwellers are buying these special places; they work long hours in the belly of the beast to spend their return keeping other people out. It is a life of exclusion—my yard, my car, my lane of traffic, and keep out of all of it.

In the past, we did not have so many members of the public with the extra jingle that two careers can bring. Some of the news from this recent change is bad. I hunt a lot of private land with the permission of my community. The new owners are strangers and prefer to remain that way. If I hunted their possession, I would take something of theirs. I'm a stranger and you're a stranger, so keep your distance and stay in your own lane.

Some of the news is good. The increased number of users has forced the creation of new plans for management of public land. A county land department used to be a storehouse for tax-forfeited parcels. Its purpose in county business was to hold the titles for the next tax-forfeit sale. Now, the land department is a revenue-producing engine of commerce. County government has learned that land returned to the taxpayer doesn't generate the same amount of revenue as land that is managed for recreation, timber, and other resources. Revenue returned to the county lowers taxes for everyone and at the same time spins off lodging, food, and fuel income for residents.

Farmers in North Dakota have discovered a new crop. They can sell the pheasants that grow in their shelterbelts and unplowed fencerows. With just a little less farming, they get more of the bird crop. Throw in some rooms and a meal, and we have the basis of fair trade—a mutually beneficial bargain.

Of course there are those who will whine about "paying for hunting." Everyone seems to know the price of everything without thinking about the value.

All we have is time, but not one of us knows how much. Every minute of every day we trade time for whatever it is that we get back. If we are sad, disgruntled, or angry, that is what we have traded for. The value of what we gave up is our life.

I am an attorney. I sell time: it takes a certain amount of my time to solve a problem, and I get paid for that time. Then, I spend the money I have earned to buy time to do what I love. Getting a fair barter, value for value, is what I seek. I spend time looking for good bird covers. In return, I receive good hunting. The price is a certain amount of my life, but the value is many times greater. On the other hand, if I am in an unfamiliar area I might buy the time of a guide. I spend the money, he gains the revenue, and I learn the country and, very likely, get some birds as a bonus.

So, whether it's time or money, public or private land, wild or tame birds, ultimately it is about one thing: a bird in the hand.